" 'Amazing grace, how sweet the sound that saved a wretch like me.' These memorable words from John Newton, could well be the subtitle of *Red Like Blood*. This book is the story of two men; one a preacher and the other an obvious sinner, who both learned to drink deeply from the gospel and to experience the amazing grace of God. *Red Like Blood* is captivating, challenging, and encouraging."

—**Jerry Bridges**, author of *The Pursuit of Holiness* and other books

"Bob and Joe shouldn't be friends. They have different backgrounds, different personalities, different stories. But in these pages you'll read the true story of a stunning event in the past that made them blood brothers for life. But be forewarned: this isn't a typical 'Christian book' where the authors wear sanitized masks and explain how to live the good life. It's an exercise in earthy honesty and gritty grace. These are guys who have seen sin up close and personal, and cannot get over being amazed by a bloody and risen and reigning Savior. Expect to be changed by reading it."

—**Justin Taylor**, managing editor of *ESV Study Bible*; blogger—"Between Two Worlds"

"So much of what purports to be Christianity fails to be real. It is *faux* Christianity: man-centered, self-atoning, conscience-easing religious therapy for those who don't want to feel needy or broken. *Red Like Blood* is real. Through the humble stories of two uncomfortably honest men you'll see the depth of your own need and you'll celebrate the Savior who meets, forgives and transforms you too."

—**Paul David Tripp**, Professor, Redeemer Seminary, Author, International Speaker

"More and more Christians are rediscovering the fact that when God saves us he doesn't move us beyond the gospel, but rather more deeply into the gospel. And this is radically re-orienting the church to the gospel's 'now-power.' *Red Like Blood* is a powerful reminder that while our daily sin reaches far, God's daily grace reaches farther. Joe Coffey and Bob Bevington beautifully demonstrate that the gospel doesn't just rescue us from our past and it doesn't just rescue us for the future—it rescues us *in the present* by regularly reminding us that in the economy of grace, brokenness always precedes usefulness."

—**Tullian Tchividjian**, Senior Pastor, Coral Ridge Presbyterian Church

"Every now and then, a book emerges that challenges and informs in ways that seem fresh and stimulating. Employing captivating stories, Coffey and Bevington speak to an audience otherwise deaf to more standard forms of communicating the gospel. The stories are thrilling in themselves, but woven into the telling of them is a gospel-thread that both entices and captivates. It is difficult to exaggerate the usefulness of this book in communicating what grace means in the lives of individuals."

—**Derek Thomas,** Professor, Reformed Theological Seminary

"What a wonderful book! I'm a cynical old preacher and sometimes have to see the 'real deal' to keep on doing what I do. This book is enough 'real deal' to last a very long time. Authenticity—incredible honesty—leaps off every page, and truth—life-changing Biblical truth—stands up and salutes. These guys 'smell like Jesus.' Read this book and you will 'rise up and call me blessed' for having told you about it."

—**Steve Brown,** Professor, Reformed Theological Seminary,
Key Life radio

"The apostle Paul defined the gospel mission very plainly, 'Christ Jesus came into the world to save sinners, of whom I am the worst.' You cannot sugarcoat sin or filter depravity, no matter what level of greatness you achieve. Joe Coffey and Bob Bevington tell their personal stories of sin and grace from the front stage of life. They pull no punches and make no excuses. Their writing is open, honest, transparent and raw. But it is not raw for the sake of shock. It is raw for the sake of hope—a saving hope—that the worst of sinners might not only find grace in the shadow of the cross, but that the darkest of lives can become examples of grace that point the worst of sinners to the gospel."

—**Greg Lucas,** author of *Wrestling with an Angel*

"Every page of incredible insight gleaned from their very candid and personal stories of faith encouraged me to walk closer to Jesus. The thought provoking, entertaining, and practical picture of a personal faith in Christ was a refreshing challenge."

—**Tom Randall,** PGA Champions Tour Chaplain,
World Harvest Ministries

Red Like Blood

CONFRONTATIONS WITH GRACE

Red Like Blood

CONFRONTATIONS WITH GRACE

Joe Coffey
AND Bob Bevington

Shepherd Press
Wapwallopen, Pennsylvania

Red Like Blood
©2011 by Joe Coffey and Bob Bevington

Trade Paperback
ISBN: 978-0-9830990-7-9

eBook
Mobi format: ISBN 978-1-936908-0-4
ePub format: ISBN 978-1-936908-1-1

Published by Shepherd Press
P.O. Box 24
Wapwallopen, Pennsylvania 18660

Page design and typesetting by Lakeside Design Plus
Cover design by Tobias' Outerwear for Books

First Printing, 2011
Printed in the United States of America

Library of Congress Control Number: 2010942555

Get an eBook of Red Like Blood at http://www.shepherdpress.com/ebooks
Kindle edition (Mobi): **RLBM01**
iPad Edition (ePub): **RLBE01**

VP   22 21 20 19 18 17 16 15 14 13 12 11
14 13 12 11 10 9 8 7 6 5 4 3 2 1

Contents

Joe and Bob

1

A Pastor's Kid and a Prodigal Become Friends

JOE

Bob was a crisp, button-down Christian. He knew a lot about the Bible and carried it to church with him every week. He was the kind of guy who could teach adult Sunday school. He had a good reputation as an eye doctor and was a pretty upstanding citizen. Then the meltdown. He had an affair with a young woman at work. He divorced his wife Rita who taught at the local Christian high school. She was diagnosed with cancer not too long after that, which made Bob an even greater pariah.

When fishermen are out for shark they do what they call "chum"—they throw bloody stuff overboard that attracts the sharks and drives them into a frenzy. Bob was a kind of Christian chum for a while. We were the sharks. What he did and how he did it pulled out all the self-righteousness in our little community. We fed on Bob for a while until we finally lost interest. Bob disappeared and when he resurfaced years later he was completely different.

I don't know if I had ever met someone so radically changed by grace. Usually you can poke someone hard enough to get them to try to defend and justify themselves. But the Bob I had known was dead, and in his place was someone else, someone I found myself desperately wanting to know. Bob Bevington has taught me about grace. I have seen it heal his relationship with Rita and with their children. I have watched as it has flowed from him into the people God brings into his life. Bob Bevington has shown me what it looks like when grace confronts brokenness.

I remember the day he called my office to make an appointment. I looked forward to the meeting since I wondered how he would defend what he had done to Rita and why he now seemed so concerned about other people's marriages. At the time, the only real contact I had with Bob was through his new wife, Amy. Amy had called to talk about a concern she had for a couple who were separating because of an affair. She said she and Bob were praying for the couple and wanted to do anything they could to help keep them together. I found that fascinating, and not in a good way.

A few days later Bob showed up at my office, sat down across from me, and leaned forward as he is prone to do. Bob is not laid back. He is an avid Ohio State Buckeye football fan and it always seems like he is ready to jump up and yell. But as we talked about how his life had blown up, he never defended himself once. Instead he asked me how I would feel if he came to my church. He rehearsed what he had done and how he had done it. He said, "Joe, I am the worst. Everyone knows it. I will completely understand if you think we should find someplace else to go to church. I'm sure it would be simpler for you, and it would probably be better for us." I realized he was making it easy for me. I could just agree with him, and we'd be done.

I thought about it for a minute. I thought of the people who had already warned me that Bob was attending. But when I looked in his eyes I saw something I have rarely seen. I saw someone who has been forgiven much and therefore loves much. It was grace I saw that day, and I told Bob I wanted him to make our church his own. For the past few years I have been able to dive into grace with Bob and it has utterly changed me. For that I'll be forever grateful.

BOB

I was hung-over the first time I met Joe Coffey. My first wife, Rita, took me to Christ Community Chapel (CCC), a church that met in a school gymnasium.[1] I remember thinking it was a funny place for a church.

Joe was the assistant pastor of the church *and* the chaplain of the school. You should know this about Joe; he's a go-getter. From what I can tell he's always been that way. He's over fifty years old and still participates in Ironman competitions. He's a man's man and a very gifted communicator. Joe gave the message that Sunday but I don't remember a word he said. But that's more a reflection on my state of mind at the time than his preaching skills.

Rita and I attended for a few Sundays and then we pretty much quit going. That was fine with me. Back then I was a strong believer in "Christianity is not a religion, it's a relationship." And back then my "relationship" didn't have much room or need or respect for church.

Rita and I were blessed with two great kids, Dave and Lauren. My career as an optometrist had taken off, plus I had become an entrepreneur on the side. For the sixteen years I was married to Rita she remained faithful to me and to the Lord, while my relationship with the Lord basically just spiraled downward. By my fortieth birthday, although I had grown wealthy in the material sense, I had become spiritually bankrupt. And without even knowing it, I had lit the fuse on a 500-megaton cluster bomb that eventually went off in an explosion of adultery and divorce that would wreak immeasurable havoc in a dozen lives, and will reverberate in the lives of generations yet unborn. I will tell a lot more about that as these chapters unfold.

Fifteen years have passed since that bomb went off. As I look back I am amazed that God did not give up on me. Instead, he

11

started sending people across my path to explain how the gospel works for scandalous sinners like me. About how grace emanates from the cross. And he gradually enabled me to see glimpses of the glorious Person of Jesus—who he is and what he did. That caused something to happen deep in my soul. Call it wonder. Call it awe. Call it gratitude. Call it a confrontation with grace.

I guess you could say I'm a prodigal come home. But believe me, the path back to the Father was not easy. In the wake of setting off that cluster bomb I found myself alienated from every Christian who had ever known me. At first I simply avoided them all. But God had other plans. Amy, my second and current wife, became a Christian and a friend invited her to a women's Bible study. At Joe's church! By then CCC had grown into a megachurch with a campus and a gym of its own, and Joe had been promoted to lead pastor. I was delighted with how Amy was benefiting from the Bible study. And the relationships she formed there were a huge blessing. Eight years later she made an announcement. She wanted us to attend Joe's church on Sundays. I said, "You've got to be kidding, my name is mud in that place."

Amy knew that was true, but she didn't see it as a problem. We had outgrown the little church we were attending—they had dismal resources for our two kids, Grace and Michael. So after six weeks of resistance and unsuccessful church shopping, I agreed to visit CCC—once.

I liked everything about the church, especially Joe's message. After the service, Amy greeted some women with small kids while I ducked a few ghosts. After all those years, my fear of facing a church community that was well informed of my history hadn't eroded very much. But during the week I prayed hard about it, and when we went back the following Sunday, Amy was excited and I could smell God in that place. I prayed some more. I decided to ask to meet with Joe. I wanted to see if he thought it would be a good idea for us to become members of Christ Community Chapel.

A week later I walked into his office and sat down for a face-to-face conversation. I reviewed the sordid litany of events, the whole awful story, even though I was fairly certain Joe was aware of it. I said, "I don't know if you remember . . ."

Joe looked me straight in the eye. He was not smiling. "Yeah, I remember."

"So don't you think it would be easier for everyone if we found someplace else to go to church?"

Joe hesitated. He bit his lip. There was a long silence. I was on the edge of my seat.

"No," he said, "I don't think that would be necessary."

Joe offered me grace that day. It was clear—he knew the easy answer to my question was "Yes, someplace else." But instead of taking the simple route, he offered me grace. And I felt it deep within my soul. Instantly I could see that Christ Community Chapel was a safe place for returning prodigals. We started attending the membership class the next week.

A year later, on our way home from a missions trip to India, I told Joe I'd take a bullet for him—and that I'd do it with a big toothy grin on my face. I meant it. Literally. I'd still do it today. Like I said, the path back to the Father has not been easy. But my pastor and friend, Joe Coffey, has been a rock for me since that day in his office. If you knew him the way I do, you'd understand.

Pastor Roland and Joan Coffey

2

Looking for God in All the Wrong Places

JOE

My dad was fifteen when he decided it was time to get laid. He has been a pastor for more than fifty years and hates it when I start his story like that. I don't blame him. But there are two reasons I like to start it that way. The first is that it's true, and the second is I think it makes God look good. My story is not much different although it should be. But I am more comfortable than ever with the idea that the worse I look the better God looks. Anyway, back to my dad.

My dad grew up poor. He's the youngest of six and his dad died when he was five. Life has never been easy on the poor and it was just as true in the 1940s as it is today. Dad had found some gratification in athletics, but it wasn't nearly enough so he thought sex might hit the spot. A certain girl had a reputation for being exceedingly accommodating so my dad asked her out. He found a secluded spot and attempted to initiate the process.

Teen sex is a little like the game of Risk. Countries are taken slowly. After each advance the dice need to be rolled again. No one knows if the game is going to end or not. Dad figured he rolled a pretty sweet number and decided to make some moves. The girl stopped him. She said she had gone to a revival meeting the previous Friday and she didn't do "it" anymore.

Augustine, even though he lived 1600 years ago in what is now Algeria, was kind of like my dad when he was young. After Christ changed Augustine's life he saw one of his old flames in town. She invited him away for a weekend of frolicking and he thanked her but turned away. She thought maybe he didn't recognize her so she said, "Augustine, it is I." He turned and smiled and said, "I know, but it is not I."

The girl who was supposed to relieve my dad of his virginity had found a new God to serve. Dad had missed the window by a week. He still remembers some sixty years later that he went home frustrated and confused, but also wondering what kind of power could generate that kind of change.

I don't even know how I discovered that story about my dad. It's hard to imagine him as a horny teenager. There is a kindness in his eyes and he talks like someone who is on familiar terms with God, if you know what I mean. Soon after that encounter with the young woman, my dad and his family moved across the state. She never knew the impact she had on him. I wonder sometimes if I will see that girl in heaven. My guess is it was a pretty lousy night for her all in all. Maybe she cried herself to sleep. I have this image of finding her in heaven and introducing myself. I'd tell her what it meant to me to have the kind of dad I had. I'd thank her for the part she played in it. If that happens, I hope it takes some of the sting out of that night for her.

My mom grew up in the hills of eastern Kentucky. She worked her whole life to get rid of the hillbilly that is deep inside her and her kin. She actually had a girlfriend who married one of the Hatfields of the infamous Hatfield and McCoy feud. My grandfather ran the company store for a coal mine. He also ran a liquor store, which in those parts unofficially disqualified your family from church. Not that my mom's family would have gone anyway.

My great Uncle Clifton was the last man hanged in Virginia. He killed his son-in-law and then later took out another man for a price. My great Aunt Derona supposedly died of a botched abortion at the tender age of fifteen. Uncle Wiley had most of his family wiped out by a bad batch of pickled corn. The great-grandfather I am named after used to go on drinking binges and would come home bragging about how many women he had slept with.

My mom is a beautiful woman who longed for something more and began to hear the whispers of God blowing through the hollow. She found her way to the back of a tiny church one night when a woman missionary came preaching a gospel as hard as gopher wood. My mom stumbled forward to ask Jesus into her heart. It was a tiny church. The women there wore their hair in buns so tight it made them look like they were squinting. This was a bone-hard Christianity, not a church of hugs and potlucks.

In the movie, *It's a Wonderful Life*, Jimmy Stewart is in a bar. The bartender describes it as a place where men drink strong drinks to get drunk fast. Mom's church was a little like that in reverse. It was a place people went to drink hard religion and go straight fast. Still, Mom struggled to understand what it meant to follow Jesus, because it didn't seem to be going very well. Depressed and desperate, she went to one of the women to ask what she should do. The lady squinted (or maybe she just looked at her, it was hard to tell) and told her to stop wearing makeup if she wanted to live the life of victory. Mom went home, took off her makeup and jewelry, looked in the mirror, and decided she was now depressed, desperate, *and* ugly.

Eventually Mom and Dad found each other and got married. Which meant Dad finally got laid. Which was a good thing because it happened the right way. And eventually all those conjugal rights resulted in a family. I am the second of three sons.

When your dad is the pastor, you grow up in church. In my case, this was no figure of speech. When I was six we actually lived in the church building for over a year. A Sunday school class met in our living room. The best thing I remember about that year was finding the refrigerator down in the basement with bottles and bottles of Welch's grape juice. For a year I unknowingly drank communion straight from the bottle. Jesus and I wouldn't be that close again for decades.

When you grow up in a church where your dad is the pastor the concept of sin is not a tough one to grasp. (Don't get me wrong—our church was not legalistic. If it had been, I don't think my mom would have done well. She's too pretty and has worn makeup ever since I can remember.) As far as I could tell, I sinned because I had an older brother. Brian was a classic first-born. He was nice, good at almost everything, and obedient to my parents, which means he was a real piece of work and drove me crazy. I, on the other hand, drank fourteen beers the first time I tasted one. But I am getting ahead of myself. I couldn't have been older than four when I was looking through the screen door at my brother as he was talking to my mom. I was pretty sure he was tattling on me about something although I could have been wrong. I remember walking in and slugging him in the stomach. My thought process was that I was going down anyway so I might as well make the most of it. My circuits never really went all the way around, which is too bad for Brian 'cause he actually is a nice guy.

⌒

My dad gave an altar call at the end of every service. I'm pretty sure I still hold the record for the most consecutive conversions. Not that I would just trot up there without thinking. I was always feeling guilty about something. In all honesty, Jesus seemed pretty comfortable with my sins. He seemed prepared for it, as if nothing I did really surprised him. What Jesus did on the cross seemed like it should easily take care of forgiving me for slugging my brother in the stomach when he wasn't looking.

Loneliness was a different deal. My family only moved three times when I was growing up, but I went to nine schools in twelve years. I was moved from Wampus Elementary to Coman Hill because the district changed. I went from Coman Hill to Whippoorwill because the district decided to change back. Whippoorwill was condemned so they moved me to Crittenden Middle School, which was under construction and only housed the fifth grade so I was moved again at the end of that year. Being lonely is exquisitely painful for a kid. It is different for an adult. As an adult you can put reasons around loneliness. It helps provide some structure. It may be a dry period for friends or relationships, but even as you think this you have hope because it is only for a period of time. For a child loneliness looks like a desert where the lone and level sands stretch far away.[2] I found loneliness to be unbearable.

While Jesus was great in dealing with sin, he seemed pretty helpless when it came to loneliness. I couldn't figure out whether it took him by surprise or if he thought sin was just more serious. But it seemed like I was on my own because loneliness was about the most serious thing in my life.

I think I was seven when I found my first Jesus substitute. I figured Jesus was pretty tied up with the whole sin thing so when it came to loneliness I called in a sub. It was recess and Chris Dighton and Alan Atamer were picking teams for a quick game of "Smear the Queer." Wikipedia defines Smear the Queer as a childhood game of tag involving an object that is held by the "it" kid until he is gang-tackled and forced to give it up. But neither Wikipedia nor political correctness had made it to our playground at that time. Chris looked at me and picked me as the second overall pick. There are few things better in the world of a ten-year-old than being drafted high in a game of Smear the Queer. I felt like I could breathe. I was looking for salvation from loneliness, and it came in the form of sport. I have been an athlete ever since. Some of the coping mechanisms we form early in life can be tough to shake. For me, this first Jesus-sub is one of those.

When Jesus was being crucified some of the Pharisees yelled up at him, "Hey, come down from the cross and we will believe in you." Jesus didn't do it. He looked down on them and prayed that God would forgive them for their ignorance. I was a lonely little boy and I looked up at Jesus and said, "Hey, come down from there and I will believe in you." He didn't. He might have looked at me, but if he did I was still lonely. So I turned away and picked up a ball. For the next decade or so, the ball would be more Jesus to me than Jesus. I think he might have prayed then that God would forgive me in my ignorance because I really didn't know what I was doing. And that was the truth.

BOB

I was not a pastor's kid and my family didn't move around a lot. From the time I was born until I left for Ohio State at age eighteen, I lived in the same tiny one-story house with yellow aluminum siding. We had one bathroom for five people, including three females. We were well aware that dad could afford a bigger house, but he didn't like the idea of keeping up with the Joneses. He'd always say, "On Orrville Avenue, I'm Jones."

We lived in a middle-class town of fifty thousand lily-white Caucasians. Dad told us we were upper-middle class. We believed him because of all the signs posted around town that read, *Cuyahoga Falls, Ohio: One of the 25 Nicest Places to Live in America*. It wasn't until I was in my twenties that my Bohemian artist friend Jeff explained why calling something *nice* was more of a slam than a compliment.

About half the people of Cuyahoga Falls were Roman Catholics. The rest were WASPs—White Anglo-Saxon Protestants. No Jews. No atheists. No blacks. For the most part, we WASPs got along fine with the Catholics, the main difference being that the Catholics ate fish on Fridays. We had a huge community swimming pool called *Water Works*. None of the kids batted an eye when blacks from surrounding cities showed up. They were kind of a curiosity to us. But our parents were scared to death that it might lead to a black family moving into their neighborhood. My dad said he liked blacks—just not on his street. And all the neighbors agreed.

One weekend in my sophomore year at Ohio State I bummed a ride home and found a strange young couple living in our house. They explained that my family had moved to a bigger house in a nicer section of town. When I got there everyone thought it was hilarious that they had moved but hadn't told me. The truth was they were scared to tell me because they knew I loved that little yellow house.

My childhood was lived under my dad's thumb. I was eight years old the night The Beatles first performed on the *Ed Sullivan Show*. I wanted to see what everyone was talking about, but my dad sent me to bed just before it started. Our house was so small I could hear the TV right through my bedroom door. I quickly came to the conclusion that The Beatles sounded like a bunch of noise. (Forty-five years later I googled it and got to watch it for the very first time. The noise finally made sense—it was all those girls crying their eyes out and screaming at the top of their lungs.) The next morning at the breakfast table my dad told me I should never like The Beatles. He said their hair made them look like girls. That was 1964, when their hair was barely over their ears.

By the time I turned ten I had found out what The Beatles actually sounded like and I became a die-hard fan. I listened to them on a 9-volt transistor radio through a single plastic earplug. My dad liked to rant about how lousy rock-n-roll was and how long hair was a badge of evil. Within a few years I wanted to have long hair, but it was completely out of the question. You could say with God all things are possible, but this was an exception. In fact, to this day I've never had long hair. But in my last year of optometry school at Ohio State I grew a beard just to show my dad that he couldn't control me anymore. And when I get old I want to grow a ponytail. And a soul patch.

I was twelve when I began to get a clue about the war in Vietnam. I stood for peace so I bought an embroidered patch of an American flag with a peace sign superimposed on it. I had my mom sew it on the right cheek of my cut-off blue jeans. I was very cool—for two days—and then my dad saw it. Off came the patch. I was steamed. I later found out this was known as the Generation Gap.

My dad was an insurance agent and he hated it. He didn't like sucking up to people so he refused to join the Kiwanis Club and play the insurance guy role. He didn't learn to play golf and never joined a country club. But he eventually succeeded in the business in spite of himself. He became a specialist in selling insurance to independent long-distance truckers known as owner-operators. I never met any of his customers until his funeral. They came out in droves. They all had stories about how my dad helped them out of a jam or took a hit for them. That was a side of my dad I wish I had seen firsthand because my dad was a disciplinarian. He ruled with an iron voice—a booming voice that shook our little house whenever someone touched his favorite pen or misplaced his scissors. I'm sure the neighbors halfway down the block could hear him. That never stopped him, but it shamed me.

There was another reason I toed the line. I was morbidly afraid of the little red paddle he swung with gusto and resolve. I think it made him feel like he was a good father. But that paddle was a constant terror to me. You didn't have to defy him to get it either. One winter evening I came home from sled-riding a little late and found myself down in the basement bent over a chair. Another time we had the new minister over for dinner. I was unaware that I ate so much that the minister probably went home a little hungry. But after he left, my awareness was raised to new heights.

After that episode I managed to escape the wrath of the little red paddle by excelling in sports and school. Back then they would whack kids in school. Never happened to me, though. Not even once. I have four kids, and I spanked the oldest one twice before deciding I just couldn't bring myself to do it ever again. I'm probably not a very good father. I'm not sure.

Joe told you how sports became his first Jesus substitute. Same here. My dad was the manager of our Little League team, the Pirates. Little League was a huge deal in our town. Back then parents weren't obsessed with self-esteem so everybody played to win. If you stunk you sat on the bench until the game was decided. All of my dad's teams won championships because he taught the fundamentals. He was a great coach. Could have been a Woody Hayes, I think. Being the coach's kid meant you had to over-earn your position. So to help me out, my dad would take me over to the schoolyard and pitch hundreds of baseballs at me. He tried his best to get the ball over the plate. But in spite of his good intentions, most of his pitches hit me. He would tell me to shake it off. That the ball was just a sack of sawdust. Or a mozzarella cheese. He would tell me that my Grandpa Bevington was a great football player who wore a leather helmet and would rub his body down with salt to make his skin tough.

My dad had a friend, an almost-famous batting coach. He's the guy who taught me how to swing. I eventually got pretty good at it. One day Grandpa Bevington came up from Florida and watched our game. I really wanted to impress him. I was playing right field because I'm left-handed and was not quite good enough at age nine to play first base. A fly ball headed in my direction. "I got it, I got it!" Clunk. Hit me square on the forehead.

That night I lay in bed listening through my bedroom door to the conversation around the kitchen table. There were no screaming girls this time so I could clearly hear my grandfather's take on my lackluster performance. His words are still etched in my mind, "Maybe the boy just isn't cut out to play baseball." I was shattered. I put my face in the pillow and started bawling my eyes out.

Apparently, muffled sound travels in both directions through cheap bedroom doors. Next thing I knew my dad was kneeling down by my bed. "I know you're a good baseball player, son." I think that was the first time I knew my dad really loved me. The next day he took me to an optometrist. After I got glasses I moved to center field and I don't think I missed another fly ball until my senior year in high school when I was so in love with Rita I didn't give a hoot about baseball anyway.

~

People say your earliest concept of God is formed by your relationship with your father. I'm not sure about that. I think church played a bigger role for me. From the time I was an infant, our family went to an Episcopal church every Sunday. It was a liberal church that taught that God loves everyone unconditionally, which to me meant you could pretty much do anything you want and get away with it—at least as far as God was concerned. I actually remember thinking that God must *not* be like my dad. The Episcopal God didn't have a booming voice. And He certainly wasn't armed with a little red paddle. That was good news.

As far as I can recall no one in that church ever opened a Bible. The place was more like a social club for middle-class Democrats and the sermons were always about social issues. They had an ornate gold cross on the altar but it was never mentioned except on Palm Sundays when they made little crosses out of palm branches. I learned how to do it. The Catholics had them, too. Easter at our church was about spring and new life. I'm pretty sure we skipped right over Good Friday.

I looked forward to fifth grade because that's when our church offered Youth Group. Married couples served as leaders and the kids met in their homes on Sunday nights. It was like group therapy for a dozen adolescent boys and girls. Very warm and fuzzy. We held what we called rap sessions. A rap session was where you *rapped* about various topics, mostly sex. One night our rap session topic was worship. Our leaders told us worship was innate—even prehistoric cave dwellers worshiped. They had us close our eyes and try to visualize what cavemen used as their object of worship. After a less-than-zen-like attempt (interrupted by a few subdued giggles) they had us open our eyes as they ceremoniously unveiled something that looked like a 10-inch statue of an erect penis. My eyes never got wider than they were in that unforgettable moment. They asked, "What does this look like?" No one would answer. "C'mon, you know, what does it look like?" No response. That's when my friend Ricky, who had flunked second grade, blurted out, "It looks like a dick! They worshiped a dick!" There was a very awkward moment as everyone stared at Ricky. And then, as if it had been rehearsed, the couple smiled and exclaimed in perfect unison, "That's right! Very good, Ricky!" There was an explosion of laughter while my friend basked in the glow of his accomplishment. It might have been the first time Ricky had shouted out a correct answer in his entire life.

I'd be interested to know what the "object" they unveiled actually was. Today, I think people could get arrested or sued for what they did. But it was the 60s and you could get away with stuff like that back then.

A month later I took a more serious position on the worshiping-caveman theory. Ricky's family had moved out to the country and my mom took me there for a visit. When we arrived, my usually lethargic friend looked like he was ready to come unglued. As our moms sat down to coffee, he whisper-shouted, "C'mon" and ran out of the house at full speed. I followed him across a field and into the woods. As I ran I wondered if he was leading me to a dead body. Suddenly he stopped, breathless, and became awestruck. He pointed to a cardboard box. A severed head? I cautiously opened it with a stick. I looked inside, and I gasped. I had never seen pictures like these. Not even in National Geographic. There were hundreds of them and I instantly desired them all.

Out of the corner of my eye, I saw Ricky's face beaming. This was my moment. "Can't leave 'em in the woods," I said, "cuz they'll rot, and there's too many for you to take 'em *all* home." Ricky was convinced. So we sat down and spent the next hour dividing the stash like an NFL draft. Then we made trades. Ricky had flunked second grade for a reason. I ended up with all the best pictures, all the most thrilling ones, all the ones in living color.

I took my half home and found the perfect hiding place in the basement rafters. And I instantly became a modern day caveman, secretly worshiping in a basement three times a day. I was eleven years old. More on that later.

⌒

Much later in life it occurred to me that my earliest concept of God was only half of the truth. He's a God of love all right, but at the same time he's a holy God of perfect justice. So there's no way around it—every sin will be punished. When I was a kid I used to watch a TV show called *The Little Rascals*. I remember a scene where a student named Alfalfa was paddling the teacher, Mr. Brown. They were behind a closed door with the class on the other side. Alfalfa would whack the teacher and then cry out so the kids would think it was Alfalfa that was being spanked. The teacher had falsely accused Alfalfa, and learned of his mistake. So to save face he was taking the kid's punishment for him.

But God didn't make a mistake about my sin. He doesn't need to save face. That's why I continually marvel at the way God the Father and God the Son worked it out for sinners like me. How the Son became veiled in human flesh, assumed my position, and took all the punishment I deserve, so that God's justice would be satisfied—every sin of those he came to save would be punished by the Father in the Son. It should have been me on that cross.

Ironically, it wasn't until I came to understand God's justice and how Jesus took my place that I began to really understand God's love. And that's when *everything* began to change. More on that later, too.

When I was forty-four, my dad called my sisters and me into his study for an announcement. He just found out he had multiple myeloma, cancer of the bone marrow. "It's terminal," he said, "but I am not upset by this news. God is going to take each of us out of our bodies at a certain time and in a certain way. If this is his time and way for me, then bring it on." I watched him live out those words to the very end. Pain would wrack his body as his vertebrae slowly disintegrated. He avoided painkillers because he wanted to be able to have meaningful conversations. It so happened that I had recently sold a couple companies and was working very little at the time. So I was able to be with him a lot. We talked a lot. We confessed a lot. We cried a lot. We talked about the Pirates. We talked about the little red paddle. We talked about the cross. Two months later, he died in a hospice center. The attendants told me that people rarely die as peacefully as my dad.

My dad had a lot of faults and I spent much of my life trying to recover from them. It wasn't until he was dying that I was able to see his strengths and feel the richness of that strength. I don't think anyone ever demonstrated greater faith in the face of death. So I have come to the conclusion that the greatest thing my dad did for me was to die.

Ironic, isn't it? It's the same with the Son of God.

3

Discovering the Shame That Sticks

JOE

Church can be a little like a virus. If you are exposed a lot as a child you can develop an immunity. In bringing up my own kids, I thought about not allowing them to go to church until they were seventeen. Every week my wife and I would go but leave them at home. And then, on their seventeenth birthday we would finally let them go and discover the wonder and the beauty of worshiping the true God. I thought maybe by staying home they would develop an immunity to television instead. Somehow I knew it wouldn't work like that so I took a risk and brought them to church every week.

I had a professor named Sig who said that second-generation Christians could have *interjects*. According to Sig, interjects are beliefs these kids swallow whole that then sit there in the belly of the soul like huge pieces of meat. Eventually the kids need to throw them up, cut them into pieces, chew them, and then swallow them back down. He said the process could be violent. I think he was right.

By the time I was ten or so I was already pretty immune. Now, that's not to say I didn't see the truth in some of the things

I learned in church. I thought the sinful nature was pretty much a lock. When I was in second grade I was transferred to Coman Hill Elementary School. I didn't really know anyone. The second day on the playground a third-grader named Sandy came up to me. Everything about Sandy was scary except for his name, which is probably what made him so surly. Anyway, Sandy came up to me and said, "I hear you think you are fast." What a weird way to start a conversation. It was obvious Sandy had not developed advanced social skills. I wasn't sure what the right answer should be so I answered honestly. I said that I might be. It was the second day on the playground and you really can't blame someone for equivocating. Sandy said, "Let's race." So we raced. Sandy smoked me. After the race he walked up to me, flashed a victory smile, and then punched me in the nose. That was all it took to convince me of the doctrine of a sinful nature.

It was later that year that I met Chris Dighton. Chris was always "old" for his age. Chris introduced me to shame. We were in the cafeteria having hotdogs for lunch. Chris put his under the table and wagged it around and everyone at our table thought it was hilarious. I laughed too. I really didn't get it but I did feel a little dirty. That was my first brush with shame. Later I would jump in and get covered with it, but at age ten I just dipped my toes in.

⌒

Sin was something that had a texture and an aftertaste. So, no matter how strong my immunity got toward church, I never could shake the doctrine of sin. And along with sin came hell. Maybe not so much the traditional image of hell but hell nonetheless.

I have watched too much TV my whole life, I think. I always preface stuff I find interesting by saying, "I was channel surfing the other day . . ." Channel surfing seems an acceptable way to watch an excessive amount of TV. If I said, "I was spending my normal two hours in front of the TV and I came across this show," it would have a completely different feel.

30

So I was channel surfing the other day and I came across a show called *Celebrity Rehab*. It features washed-up celebrities in a detox center trying to kick addiction and find their path to sobriety. It never seems to occur to anyone that being a celebrity is probably an addiction, too. Their guide is Dr. Drew who seems pretty gifted although becoming more and more of a celebrity himself. I watch week after week as these poor souls struggle to break free. It's apparent that methamphetamine, crack, and even alcohol can result in a quick disintegration. The lives of these celebrities have come completely unglued due to their addiction and they've destroyed nearly all their relationships in the process. They are isolated and still craving the substance that has made them so lonely. They sometimes describe themselves as being in hell. I think in some ways they are right.

God made us for himself. *Anything* I put in his place is bound to be less than what I need there in my soul. So I demand more and more of it and consume more and more of it, until I develop a full-blown addiction to it. Eventually I become bloated with it and when it runs its course it makes me come apart at the seams. The problem with most of our addictions is they are slow-acting and the disintegration may not even be noticeable at first. The man with the job that keeps his mind whirling through the night doesn't think of himself as an addict. The woman who sits up and worries all the time about her children thinks of herself only as a good mom, not an addict. But if I take this mother and extrapolate her life out hundreds or even thousands of years, all that will be left of her will be a quivering bag of anxiety. A living hell.

I watch *Celebrity Rehab* and I see people who desperately need God. Without him, the best they can possibly do is replace one habit with another. Cheetos for Cocaine. What then? Next I think of all the people who are addicted to slow-acting things like success and relationships and family. Hell is being dependant for your life on something that cannot deliver. It's the result of what Frederick Buechner said was "the craving for salt by a man who is dying of thirst." I not only see that truth on television,

I feel it deep down in my soul. So I have always been a believer in both sin and hell.

Bob was eleven when his friend Ricky introduced him to pornography. He disappeared into a cave and my guess is he stayed there throughout adolescence. I understand completely. As a teenager I was on fire. I don't mean on fire like a basketball player gets when he makes every shot he takes. I mean the fire that only pure natural testosterone can kindle in a young man's loins. I have never heard it described as well as Buechner does in his book, *Godric*.[3] "Lust is the ape that gibbers in men's loins. Tame him as you will by day he rages all the wilder in our dreams by night. Just when we think we're safe from him, he raises up his ugly head and smirks, and there's no river in the world flows cold and strong enough to strike him down. Almighty God, why dost thou deck men out with such a loathsome toy?"

I remember trying to do everything I could to control that gibbering ape. I thought if I ever got lust under control then living like Jesus would pretty much be a cakewalk. I always thought the temptations Satan used on Jesus in the desert were a little weak. Why didn't he stumble up to an oasis and find Pamela Anderson sunbathing? Taking a swan dive off the pinnacle of the temple doesn't seem to hold a candle to Pamela Lee. But I found out that lust wasn't my real problem. Lust is just a symptom.

I swim for exercise. On swim days I itch. And before long I overscratch. I find that scratching an itch really feels good. It feels so good I continue to scratch and it's only when I quit scratching that I realize I've actually started to bleed a little. I'm not bleeding much but there it is on my leg or my arm and instead of an itch I now have pain. I do the same with eating sometimes. I am hungry so I eat but then eating feels good so I overeat. As weird as it sounds, I think the reason I do these things is that I am not home yet. The itch reminds me that something is not quite right here in this world. Life can be good and yet I itch. It's an itch that is deep down in my soul where it's hard to reach. Lust is one of the ways I would try to scratch that itch. The formerly famous people on *Celebrity Rehab* itch. Fame might have been scratching that itch for a while. Then it was drugs. Dr. Drew is trying to get them to quit scratching so hard. But what about the itch?

Martin Luther wrote that no one breaks any of the laws of God until they break the first commandment. We move away from God and we begin to itch. If I write long enough about itching you will put this book down so you can start scratching. And so it is. All the other commandments are about different ways to scratch. Jesus came and walked the earth and never got itchy. It fascinated the sinners and drove the Pharisees crazy. I picture Jesus standing there teaching and everyone listening and scratching, scratching and listening.

I think the garden of Gethsemane was the first time Jesus could feel the itch coming. Later on the cross, it became unbearable. The Bible says his blood did many things that day. All of them are wonderful things. But on the days when I really understand the cross the thing I feel deep down is this: His blood has taken away my itch. It is interesting to me that there is blood either way. When I feel the itch deep down I can scratch until I bleed or I can go to the cross where his blood takes my itch away.

BOB

There's a log cabin I head to whenever I want to get away and think. I call it Walden Pond because it looks like a scene from Thoreau. There's no electricity so some nights I read by candlelight and think of Abraham Lincoln. The cabin has a tin roof so thunderstorms sound like a percussion orchestra of marimbas, tympani, and cymbals. Many times I thought I was experiencing a taste of heaven in the solitude there. God is everywhere, but he often seems especially close at Walden Pond.

The cabin is located on the grounds of a hunting and fishing club. They raise pheasant, quail, and partridge in half-acre cages and then release them around the 500-acre property. Then on special days they hunt them down. I participated in this process once. Between the dogs and the shotguns, the poor birds didn't stand a chance. That night we attended the Annual Wild Game Dinner and I discovered you could eat an entire quail breast in a single bite. At one point my molars clenched down on a piece of buckshot that sent a jolt of electricity through my brain. Ever since that day I've stuck to fishing. But mostly I just hang out at the cabin and enjoy the solitude.

The club is also known for its sporting clay courses. I tried that once, too. You shoot little orange Frisbees out of the air. It's fun but the shotguns are so loud you have to wear ear protectors. I can even hear them a half-mile away at Walden Pond. Some days I get annoyed and think, *What's wrong with this picture?* I keep lots of earplugs handy. But every so often I just sit on the porch, close my eyes, and listen to the gunshots. Sometimes I see glorious fireworks bursting on the back of my eyelids. Other times my mind drifts back to old war movies where wives and kids are hiding from the Nazis as tanks and howitzers blast everything outside their windows into smithereens. Sometimes I remember my visit to The Holocaust Museum in Washington, D.C., where I saw thousands of empty shoes and bales of human hair on display. Shoes and hair that used to be worn by real people—men, women and children. It's like I'm standing there again, dumbfounded, and world history seems like an unbroken chain of wars and injustices, extending all the way back to Cain and Abel.

But the little things of the world and the best things of the world are also broken. Did I mention the mosquitoes at Walden Pond? Between howitzers by day and bombardment by mosquitoes the size of bats by night, the idyllic serenity is interrupted every five minutes. So even at Walden Pond it's evident that something's gone very wrong with the world.

My friend, Jay Volk, is quite the pacifist. He wears a blue wristband that says, *Wage Peace.* He would not be happy with me if he knew I kept a handgun at home. I previously kept it in my safe deposit box until one day I casually mentioned it to the bank manager. She asked me how I got the gun into the bank. That's when we both realized I had strolled into a bank with a firearm and a couple hundred rounds of ammo. "Don't worry,"

I reassured her, "it isn't loaded," which was actually true since the bullets were still in the boxes. A week later I smuggled all of it back out of the bank. I'm not really sure why I keep my gun. Part of me wants to give it to Jay so he can have it melted down and hammered into a plowshare. But another part of me wants to keep it to protect myself and my family from a broken world.

⌒

I didn't know Jay during the Vietnam War. But he'd have been proud of me. Back then Uncle Sam could draft you into the Army and if you didn't report you would end up in prison. The draft was based on a lottery system. They sent you a number on your eighteenth birthday—the lower the number, the better your chances of going to Vietnam. By 1974 no one could give me a good reason for American soldiers being in Vietnam. Over fifty thousand of them had perished by that time, and I couldn't see the point in giving my life to add to that number. So I sent away for a Conscientious Objector's Handbook. After looking it over I made up my mind; I was going to Canada if I had to. I told my parents and to my utter amazement they approved. When my birthday came and I got #235 I was actually a little disappointed, because that meant instead of a becoming a draft-dodging rebel with a cause in need of amnesty, I was destined to become a college student with an attitude in need of a high grade point average. Thus ended my brief tenure as a political activist.

Thirty-five years later I went to visit my wealthy friend who lives near Washington, D.C.. He hired a driver and took me on a tour I will never forget. Our first stop was the Vietnam War Memorial. It's a stark black granite wall inscribed with the names of more than 58,000 Americans, listed in chronological order by date killed. I looked at the last guy who died and wished he had gone to Canada. It was Kelton Rena Turner, an eighteen-year-old Marine. He was killed in action on May 15, 1975—the day I prepared to return home for summer break after my freshman year at Ohio State.

It was dark when we arrived at the Jefferson Memorial, but it was spectacularly lit up inside and out. I looked into the eyes of the larger-than-life bronze statue of America's third President and I felt like I somehow knew him. Then I read his famous quotes that circled the room. They were all about freedom—American freedom from the British Empire. At the Lincoln Memorial the message was the same—God-endowed, inalienable rights. Life, Liberty, and the Pursuit of Happiness. Freedom for all, including the slaves. I suddenly felt connected to America. As we headed to Georgetown for a glass of merlot, I was swollen with patriotic pride.

On the way we drove past a statue of an old, hunched-over Indian chief. It reminded me there are cracks in the ideals I had just read about. Cracks big enough for whole races to fall through. In the 60s, the Civil Rights Movement identified the injustices done to the Native Americans, but as far as I know all we've ever done for them is give them some useless land and build them some second-rate casinos. I remember in *Blue Like Jazz*, Donald Miller and his friends put up a booth on the campus of Reed College and confessed the sins of the Crusades.[4] I think some of the things we Christians have allowed to happen on this soil need to be confessed. Maybe Joe and I should set up a booth over at Kent State.

Jay once told me he would not take up arms and resist if terrorist insurgents invaded our country. I think there are things Jay would die for, just nothing he would kill for. I understand that but I still have my little handgun just in case a situation comes up that Jay hasn't thought about.

Jay is the president of a successful software company. He has a unique business card. Underneath his name, instead of saying "President" it says, "One Happy Fella." It's true that Jay always has an optimistic smile on his face. But one day when it looked like his company might go down the tubes, I saw a distant sadness beneath his habitual smile. No one is immune to the brokenness. Not even Jay the Pacifist.

Everywhere you look, the world is broken. From Walden Pond, to Vietnam, to the Holocaust, to the Great Frontier, to the

Crusades, to Cain and Abel, and back around to me, Jay and Joe, nations are broken and individuals are broken. Things are not as they should be.

⌐⁓⌐

I have found that I am like a balloon. I inflate quite easily, meaning it doesn't take much to make me feel like I am better than everyone else. It never has. And I am never more dangerous than when I am feeling good about me.

I was flying high in the sixth grade because of school and sports and mostly because I had the cutest girlfriend on the face of the earth. One day our bald and muscular gym teacher, Mr. Boyle, picked me as his partner to take on the entire sixth grade in dodgeball. That alone started my balloon inflating. And when we actually beat them three times in a row, my balloon couldn't have possibly held more air. I proceeded to the locker room, found the weakest kid in the school, and repeatedly snapped him with a towel while the other kids laughed. He was naked and wet from the shower. That kid was known for only one thing—a very bad case of psoriasis or eczema or both. Scaly brown skin covered most of his body. Ironically, he also had the misfortune of having a matching name, Mark Weltyde. When I was done tormenting him with the towel, I christened him, *Marks of Welted Hide*.

As soon as I walked out of the locker room, Mr. Boyle called me into his office. I cringe when I think of how cocky I was in this next part. I actually sauntered into his office, saluted, and said, "Bob Bevington reporting for duty, sir!" I must have thought he wanted to talk about us taking on the sixth grade in a tug-of-war. Instead, he told me he was ashamed to find out how I treated Mark. My balloon instantly popped and my body went limp. He told me to think about it and I've done that for more than forty years. But amazingly I still inflate almost as fast as ever.

I have never forgotten Mark or Mr. Boyle or what an ass I can be. I apologized to Mark within the hour, but not the way I would today. For the next couple years, I attempted to make up for the locker room episode by treating Mark like a brother. I protected him from all lurking dangers. And I grew to like him. He was kind and gentle. And he could be funny. I wish I could find him. If you can help me with that, I'd appreciate it.[5] But here's my point. I learned early in life that I am capable of being a very, very crappy person.

I have an elderly patient who likes to dress up and come in for a chat. The eye exam is secondary. She updates me on her latest family news and shows me pictures. She has dozens of grand-children and several great-grandchildren. One day she showed up and was not very talkative. I thought maybe she was actually concerned about her eyes. "My eyes are fine," she responded. So I asked, "You feeling okay?" "No. Not really." She went on to tell me her oldest grandson was in deep trouble. He was in jail and she couldn't believe it because he was a Christian and had never done anything wrong in his life. She began to weep. Her hand shook as she reached into her purse and took out a picture of her latest great-grandson. "Haven't you read the papers?" That's when she broke down and became inconsolable. My assistant rescheduled her appointment while I slipped into the lunchroom to see the newspaper. The headline: Father Shakes Baby Son to Death.

I immediately had a flashback. The wee hours of a night twenty years prior when, exhausted and sleep-deprived and angry because Rita refused to get up, I stormed into the nursery and found myself within a hair's breadth of shaking my own son.

I exchanged letters with that young man while he was in jail awaiting his sentencing. He said he didn't mean to do it. He just had one real bad moment. He said he was ready to accept the consequences, which was a good thing because he got life in prison, with no chance of parole for fifteen years. His wife divorced him, sued him, and swore he would never see their two other children. There, but for the grace of God, go I. And I shudder to know it's true.

The world is broken and you and I are broken for the same reason: sin. Our sins fly under the banner of a Declaration of Independence from God. They are acts of cosmic treason in which we disregard God and put other gods in his place. I began consciously worshiping other gods at eleven and have been rotating gods in ever since.

Ultimately, our displays of sin reveal the fact that although we say we love God, we love ourselves more. We fail to uphold his glory because we want it for ourselves. Our default mode is self-centeredness, not God-centeredness. Our sins throw us out of tune, out of touch, and eventually out of joy and out of hope because we are not doing what we were created to do. We're sad and disappointed, and our relationships are messy. Our happiness, pleasure, and contentment are either artificial or short-lived or both. And collectively we account for the brokenness of the world.

Only Jesus lived a sinless life, so only Jesus was perfectly whole. Jesus never failed to love the Father. Jesus never hid any secret objects of worship in the rafters of a basement. He never inflated like a balloon. He could look his enemies in the eye and say, "I always do the things that are pleasing to the Father."[6]

Jesus hung on the cross where his body was broken so that our souls could be made whole. Not only was his body broken for us, his relationship with the Father was broken as well. Why? So that our relationship with a holy God could be restored forever. We are accepted, approved, and blessed by God on behalf of another—Jesus, Son of God and Son of Man. He's my Savior. He's my hope. Even if I had shaken my son to death and spent the rest of my life in prison, he's my hope.

What if I could stand in for the young father in prison? I didn't shake my son to death but if I could substitute for him and serve his sentence—that would be grace. That's what Jesus did for me. He stands in to take the condemnation and punishment for what I did to Mark Weltyde. Jesus didn't snap the towel and yet he bore the guilt. He bore the guilt for all the times I have been dangerous because of my inflated balloon, for what I did to Rita, Dave, and Lauren, for all of it.

Daniel the Leper Pastor

4

The Appearance of the Unseen God

JOE

When I was three, I stood on a folding chair in front of a microphone and sang for the church. The song was "Untold Millions are Still Untold." I didn't even have a band, just Mrs. Petersen on the piano. It was the evening service, but even in that lesser venue I could tell I was a star. People raved. It was my first taste of the strongest elixir the world has ever known, the feeling of being someone special. The problem is it takes some doing to actually become someone special. It takes a sort of magic if you ask me.

When I was ten, I remember practicing my autograph just in case I ever became famous. If people were going to stand in line for hours to get me to sign something for them the least I could do was give them a signature that would be a pleasure to look at. So I practiced. I did all kinds. I filled up whole notebooks with autographs. To be honest, my signature stunk. I have a name with plenty of good letters. There is no reason why Joe Coffey should not look elegant and cool. But it has always looked dorky and inconsistent, which is why I am probably not famous still.

41

People are wispy. Most of us know it. A teenager stands by her locker and if her friends aren't around she might as well be invisible. I pick on a teenager but we are all like that. There is a longing to be solid. You can be in a crowd and feel invisible until someone calls your name—the sound of your name makes you appear. A friend who knows your name can make you solid. That is a kind of magic as well.

I don't have Tourette's syndrome but I am pretty sure my wife thought I had it right after we got married. Tourette's is a disease that diminishes impulse control. If you have it you could shout out completely inappropriate things. At times I think it would be a handy diagnosis to have.

About a month after my wife and I were married, I was trying to explain what was going on in my head. I have always felt that romantic love was a fairly unstable emotion. I had been "in love" a couple of times before my wife. I remembered one of my professors saying that "like" was a much better reason to get married than "love." It made sense to me but the fact is I married my wife because I was madly in love with her and felt like I was going to explode if we didn't get married. Anyway, about a month into the marriage I decided to tell her how my feelings for her had stabilized and how that was a really good thing. I told her that I didn't think I loved her as much as I really *liked* her now. That is when she looked at me as if she wished I had Tourette's. I backtracked and told her that it meant I loved being with her. I put Love in every sentence for the next hour. It didn't help.

I still think my intent was good. I was trying to tell her that I knew her better now than ever before. My feeling of love had been based on some strange concoction of who she was, who I thought she was, how I saw myself when I was with her, and a couple of shots of sexual energy. After a month of marriage it had been distilled down to just her and what I felt was deep affection.

My friend David is from New Jersey. That pretty much makes him a candidate for Tourette's right there. He told me he grew up

42

hearing about the love of God. He knew God loved him but he never felt that God liked him very much. He finally read a book where the author talked about having a breakthrough with God. He said that if Jesus was here on earth it struck him that Jesus would want to hang out with him. That flipped a switch in my friend Dave. It took God liking Dave to convince Dave that God loved him. And so it is. It worked with Dave but take my advice, don't try it with your wife.

⁓

Love is fraught with all kinds of problems. The most fundamental problem is that my deep need to feel loved is in direct conflict with my deep fear of being known. For Bob the tough part of coming to our church was that he was known. Most of us can avoid having our worst sins displayed for all to see. But Bob's adultery was hung out like clothes on a clothesline—everyone in our church knew the color of his skivvies. Almost everyone I know is hiding in one way or another but Bob has been outed. It should have destroyed him and in some ways it did. But in the midst of that death came a life that swallowed him up whole. Maybe that is why Bob feels the love of God so deeply. The rest of us all long to be known but just can't muster the courage to out ourselves.

I am not telling you anything you do not already know. You have felt deep down that longing to be loved and that fear of being known. It is like being made to live in water and not being able to swim. If you really know me, will you love me? I doubt it because, put in your place, I wouldn't love me either. I long for the experience of really being loved and yet all I give is the image of myself I hope others will find most attractive. The love I feel from others is muted at best, simply because I know that the person they love is not the person I am. Inside of me are smaller and smaller me's until there is one that is so small and homely that it never feels the love it craves. I merely pretend to be me so I can pretend to be loved, and I starve.

The most amazing thing about the gospel is that God claims to know the smallest me, the small troll-like me that never comes out into the light. And he loves me in spite of myself. Jesus didn't stand at the mouth of the cave and call me out like Lazarus. Instead, Jesus came all the way down into the cave to sit with me in the darkness. When Jesus does that there's nowhere to run.

It's one thing to know the facts about the gospel. I have known since I could walk the story of the crucifixion and resurrection of Jesus. It's quite another to experience the truth of the gospel in the core of who you are. I was in a 1968 Volkswagen Beetle when I felt Jesus come into my cave. As far as I could tell he had never been in there with me before. I drove for over an hour with him sitting in the midst of my darkness. He never flinched. He just sat there until I was convinced he loved me. I remember hearing someone say that most Christians only pretend to be sinners so they can only pretend to be forgiven. Ever since that day in the Volkswagen, I have never been able to pretend again. And every time I see a Beetle I smile and remember the moment I felt loved and known at the same time. I have never been the same. There is a magic there as strong as any.

When I was twenty-five, I led a six-week mission trip to Bolivia. My brother Brian and I had both played basketball in college so we got a team together and went down to Bolivia to play and preach. There was one stage of the trip that was absolutely grueling. In a thirty-hour stretch we played three games, had one meal, and slept for a total of about four hours. We were dehydrated and some of us were battling serious dysentery. In the movie, *A Few Good Men,* when Tom Cruise asked Jack Nicholson if Private Santiago was in "grave danger," Jack responded with the classic, "Is there any other kind?" That is the way I feel about dysentery. The kind I had was grave. We were just about to board a train for an all-night trip when I had to go. Train station restrooms in Bolivia in the 80s were about as terrible as you can imagine. Got a picture in your mind? It was worse. There was a toilet but it had no seat and it didn't flush. It was nasty. I decided it was best to try to do my business without actually having my body touch anything. As I hovered over the porcelain my legs cramped and I fell in. I yelled for my friend Moose to pull me out. I tried to clean up the best I could and boarded the train.

We were heading from the town of Uyuni to the town of Wanuni in the southern mountains of Bolivia. The windows of the train would not close completely and the mountain air was thin and frigid. About three in the morning I was drifting in and out of twilight sleep when I thought I heard someone crying. As I started to emerge into consciousness I recognized it was the sound of a man crying. I was curious so I just listened for a while. But as I slowly became more awake I realized that the one who was crying was me. I was sitting next to my brother, leaning against his body for warmth and whimpering like a little girl. It was pitiful. I have never been more miserable.

As we arrived in Wanuni we knew the accommodations would be similar to those in Uyuni. Why should they be any different? There would be a single floor with several tiny rooms, a central bathroom with no hot water, and big thick dusty quilts on the bed. In Uyuni we'd had the heaviest quilts I have ever seen, but they were absolutely useless against the cold. Brian and I sent the team ahead and waited at the train station for the last taxi. We stood without talking and then rode in silence to the boarding house. We rounded a corner and saw a five-story hotel. It looked like a mirage. There were big block letters lit up on top of the building. They read, "HOTEL TERMINAL." I elbowed my brother and said, "Do you see that?" He was speechless. We walked into the lobby and signed an old-fashioned registration book and headed to the first elevator we had seen in weeks.

Our room had its own bathroom. I walked into the bathroom and pulled back the shower curtain. There were two knobs. One for cold water and one for hot. I had not seen two knobs in six weeks of travel. I turned the hot knob and steaming water shot out. I couldn't believe it. I heard shouts down the hall as the other guys made the same discovery. After long, hot showers we gathered in the hotel restaurant for steak and eggs. It was there around the tables we began to talk about the night before. We talked about how I had fallen into the toilet, how bad it smelled, how cold it was in the train, and the weird sound of a grown man crying. We laughed until the tears rolled down our cheeks.

In the *Lord of the Rings* trilogy there is a scene where Sam Gamgee comes across Gandalf and is shocked to see him alive. He says, "I thought you were dead." And then he thinks again and says, "but then I thought I was dead myself." And finally he says, "Is everything sad going to come untrue?" Heaven is not a place where there is simply no more pain. It is a place where all sad things are redeemed. The trip to Hotel Terminal was terrible. I have never been more miserable. But I have never laughed harder than I did at breakfast the next morning. And the things we laughed hardest about were the very things that had made us so miserable the night before.

My little brother John was killed in a motorcycle accident. He hit a truck head-on. One day I expect to sit with him in heaven and laugh until the tears roll down our faces about how hard he hit that truck. Making all sad things come untrue is the greatest magic of all.

BOB

To me, almost everything is magic. I say *almost* because there are some things that seem magic, but if you look beneath the surface, you find something like anti-magic. Take my town's Fourth of July fireworks. A high-budget fireworks display set to Tchaikovsky's *1812 Overture* can almost take my breath away. But at the end of the grand finale, the inevitable earsplitting blasts remind me that the freedom we are celebrating has a direct connection to hundreds of thousands of real people screaming as their lifeblood spills out on a battlefield somewhere. It's then that what seemed like pure magic implodes and its impure side is exposed.

I was channel-surfing one day when I was depressed. This is not a pseudo-confession that I watch a ton of TV like Joe. I only watch it when I'm depressed or when Ohio State is playing football and I don't have tickets. By the way, in case you are wondering, Michigan is not in my vocabulary.

Anyway, I landed on a show that exposed the secrets of big-stage magicians. It turns out that levitating people and making buildings disappear are pretty simple tricks. There's no magic in magic. That discovery made me even more depressed, so I turned the TV off and went outside. The night sky was clear. I looked up and noticed I could see all nine stars of the Pleiades. The depression lifted a little, so I lay down on my back in the wet grass and attempted to drink it all in: the inconceivable vastness of the universe, the innumerable celestial bodies, their diversity and beauty. "God," I said aloud, "You are quite the magician." Suddenly I felt really small, and my problems seemed even smaller. Before long I realized that the Great Magician had actually made my depression disappear.

I have several habits you would find weird. For example, I look at my hand and move my fingers. This will go on for a minute or two at a time. Whenever I catch people catching me doing this, it's obvious they think I'm a lunatic. But that hasn't deterred me from doing it almost every day, even in crowded places in broad daylight. Because it's an extraordinary phenomenon. Go ahead and try it. It's amazing, isn't it? How in the world does it work? It's like magic. Are we making it happen? Who could design a thing like this? To me, it's living proof that there is a God. And as I watch my fingers move, I feel like somehow I'm in synergy with the Creator. Inevitably, before long, I am in awe of God because it dawns on me anew that his magic is pure magic.

I studied chemistry in college and quickly discovered the similarities between atoms and solar systems. Atoms have tiny nuclei with little electrons orbiting around them, and solar systems have giant suns with whole planets orbiting around them. That was a cool observation, but reading about sub-atomic particles really got my head spinning. I marveled at the fact that no one really understands the forces that hold atoms together. There are wave theories and particle theories and particle-wave theories. But if they're being honest, scientists will admit they don't have much of a clue about how it works.

One sunny spring afternoon in my sophomore year I became exhausted from the dog-eat-dog world of my pre-med "weed-out" courses. So I headed to The Oval—a lawn the size of six football fields in the middle of the Ohio State campus. I went there with nothing but a Bible. I sat down Indian-style and tried to count the Frisbees that seemed to be flying around everywhere. I imagined I was sitting on a neutron and the Frisbees were undiscovered subatomic particles. Half in a daze I opened the Bible to Colossians chapter 1. Within seconds I was jolted out of my chemistry-induced stupor. After introducing God's "beloved Son" as "the image of the invisible God," it says that, "by him all things were created, in heaven and on earth, *visible and invisible . . . all things* were created through him and for him. And he is before all things. . . . " Then came the clincher, "*and in him all things hold together.*"[7] I was dumbfounded. It's far more than just a plausible explanation. Divine Magic holds atoms and molecules and solar systems and galaxies together. And the magic is a Person.

⌒

Getting back to the planet Earth for a while, let me share something I've noticed about magic in relationships. You've noticed it, too. There's more magic in giving than in receiving. One day in India, our medical team was in a hot, dusty, rural village serving hundreds of the poorest of the poor and sweating like we were in a sauna. Out of the corner of my eye I saw an old dark-skinned man trying to get my attention. I knew he was begging so I resisted making eye contact (a skill I honed when I lived in New York City). I was trying to wipe the sweat out of my eyes when I inadvertently looked right at him. He wanted my shoes. I thought, "I can't give my shoes to every Tom, Dick and Patanjali that wants them. Besides, I shouldn't be walking around barefoot in this filthy dust." I quickly looked away and that's the last I saw of him.

When the grueling day was over, our team headed to the shuttles. That's when I saw Ken Ellingsen walking barefoot. I stared at his feet. They were as dusty as my shoes. Ken's eyes were weary but bright with magic. Mine were red and getting wet with shame. For me it was a long ride back to the mission station. Joe is fond of saying that joy is the currency of the kingdom of God. Ken was shoeless and loaded with joy. And I was as broke as the day was long. The others chatted and laughed while I silently pondered once again the anti-magic inside me. It wouldn't be the last time. It rises up when I least expect it.

On my second trip to India I served as an assistant to my good friend Brad. He's a skilled videographer and our assignment was to capture the essence of the ministry of the India Gospel League. My job was to interview people by asking questions off-camera. One day the two of us fed about fifty lepers, which in itself was a deeply moving experience. I recognized one of them from my first trip. His name was Daniel—he was both a pastor and a leper. He had an unforgettable face—half of his nose had been eroded away by leprosy. The translator knew him, too, and asked Daniel if we could interview him. Little did I know that I was about to come face-to-face with some of the strongest magic I've ever encountered.

I began the interview with a statement. "We understand that in India it is believed that lepers are under the curse of a god. So how does it feel to know Jesus as your curse-bearer?" After a long pause, the answer came back though the translator: "Jesus Christ is all I have." I nodded my head knowing it was literally true. Daniel owned nothing. Yet his eyes betrayed a deep contentment and joy rarely seen in Americans. To be honest, I was stunned and couldn't think of a follow-up question. But Daniel spoke again, "Jesus Christ is all I need." Six more little words that spoke volumes and I knew he was revealing authentic secrets of pure magic! He looked at me, waiting patiently for me to respond, but I was speechless. I started to pray silently, asking for God's help. Just then Daniel began to speak a third time. My eyes were riveted on his face as the words flowed from the translator like magic arrows penetrating deep into my soul, "Jesus Christ is all I want."

That night Brad and I talked into the wee hours. I told him I was jealous of Daniel's faith. And that I was sad because I knew my faith could never be as pure as his because I have too many things propping me up. Brad sat back and listened to me go on and on. Finally he said quietly, "You are right . . . unless someday you are in the process of dying and one-by-one everything is being taken away." Ironic, isn't it? But true.

———

There's another irony that is overflowing with magic. Grace. God's blessings in Christ toward those who deserve his curse for their sin. It's ironic that God offers grace in the first place. But it's even more ironic *how* he makes it ours. Tim Keller writes in *The Prodigal God*, "The prerequisite for receiving the grace of God is to know you need it."[8]

In the Sunday night Bible study that meets in our basement we put it like this: "Our brokenness forms the cracks through which grace flows in." We should know. We are a rag-tag band of train-wrecked lives. Nearly all of us have had major self-induced catastrophes of one kind or another. Divorce, career meltdowns, addictions, and shockingly prideful rebellion. And all of us admit to being broken every day because we continue to sin and fall short of the glory of God. As a result, we are desperate for the gospel. So each week we remind ourselves of the Good News that we can take all our brokenness, all our sin, to the cross—the unfailing source of God's grace. And almost every week, by the time we end in prayer, most, if not all of us, experience some magic. To us there is nothing more magical than experiencing the reality of grace.

By definition, grace is an undeserved blessing. The ultimate blessing is that because of who Jesus is and what he did, we get God. First Peter 3:18 says, "For Christ also suffered once for sins, the righteous for the unrighteous, *that he might bring us to God . . .*" Let this verse sink in. Jesus, as the perfect sin sacrifice, trades our unrighteousness (sin) for his righteousness. And as a result, we get God—he accepts us on behalf of Jesus. The God we get is the Master Magician: the fountain of every good and perfect gift.[9] He is the most glorious, majestic, interesting, satisfying Person in the universe. He is perfectly holy. He loves sinners at an infinite cost to himself. He is incomparable. The apostle John knew Jesus as well as any man on earth. When he was old he wrote this:

"That which we have seen and heard we proclaim also to you, so that you too may have fellowship with us; and indeed our fellowship is with the Father and with his Son Jesus Christ."[10]

The older I get the more I realize that all the magic I have, all the magic I need, and all the magic I could ever want is right at my fingertips because of the gospel. The ultimate magic is fellowship with the Father and the Son. Fellowship happens when we actually *experience* the reality that we have God here and now. I have so little of it. I'm no Daniel the Leper. My faith is small so my experience of fellowship is shaky at best. But I do have some exquisite moments. Father, Son, and Holy Spirit initiate them all. It's all of grace. And it's all pure, unadulterated magic.

Tim Elliott

5

Truth, Reality, and the Riding of Our Lies

JOE

I have always wanted to be profound. When I was in college I memorized an obscure poem because it sounded so deep. I still remember it.

> What's real isn't real at all and
> what seems a fortress is about to fall.
> And nothing lasts except for forever.
> But dreams do come true so dream on dreamer.

Every once in a while I would bring it out at a party to impress my friends with something deep about reality. Today, I can't imagine why anyone would have been impressed. But somehow the people I hung out with thought it was pretty good. I think it was mostly because it had the word "real" in it. Everyone wants to be on the inside lane with being true and real but all of us struggle to stay there. We want to stay there, but most of the time we know we are just not very good at tracking with either reality or truth. Here we are living every day smack in the middle of this 3D, five-senses, time-and-space world, and we still have an amazing amount of trouble with what's real and true.

I have counseled a lot of people during my time as a pastor. People tell themselves lies all the time. Each lie is like a thin string, like a cobweb. By the time they come into my office they are like Spiderman gone berserk. They are covered in webs. Every once in a while sin hits them so hard it knocks all the webs off and they stand there naked before the truth. It is their only shot at being free.

I used to lead mission trips to the Dominican Republic. During training I would always warn my team to stay away from the water. I'd drill it into them. "Only drink bottled water. Don't open your mouth in the shower. Don't brush your teeth with tap water. Don't let a single drop slide down your throat or it will scream to get out of every orifice. Do. Not. Drink. The. Water." Most of the time everyone listened. Almost.

Randy had just graduated from college. He was in the best shape of his life. He was smart, good looking, and built like a brick house. One day he left the construction site where we were building an orphanage. When he came back his lips were red. I asked him about that. He told me he had just had a snow cone. I said, "You had a snow cone? You mean from a street vendor?" He said, "Yeah, and it was great. It must be 100 degrees right now. I never tasted anything so good." I believed that part. I said, "Randy, you know a snow cone is made of ice and there is quite a bit of water in ice if I remember right." He said, "That's okay, I feel great." I said, "Yeah well, Randy you are a dead man walking right now. You are done." Randy could not get himself to believe me. He felt so good and the snow cone had been so refreshing. How could something so good be so wrong? I happened to be rooming with Randy. The next morning I woke up and Randy was on all fours by my bed. He looked up at me and in a raspy, barely audible voice said, "Just kill me." Reality had broken through and Randy would feel it shooting out of him for the next four days.

My wife and I went to an AA meeting once. It wasn't even our date night. It was held in a bingo parlor in a seedy part of town. As we walked up to the building we were greeted warmly by the half dozen men who were grabbing their last smoke before things got started. At our church we have official greeters. These guys didn't strike me as official. They weren't hoping we would come back and make their meeting our home meeting. But they recognized we were new and it seemed they genuinely wanted us to feel welcome. We went inside and I looked around the hall and saw people from just about every walk of life. I take that back. Every walk of life *that* group of people had been on must have been hard. I could see the pain and the wear and tear on their faces. Some more than others, but it was unmistakable in all of them. The interesting thing was that no one tried to hide it.

The meeting started and the emcee introduced himself. "Hi, I'm Stan and I'm an alcoholic." People replied, "Hi, Stan." Someone else made the same introduction and got the same response. And so it went for the next hour. As far as I could tell there wasn't a cobweb in the place. These people seemed like they had already used up their lifetime quota of lies and now they gathered in this room and took turns stepping out into the light.

At the end of the meeting we stood in a big circle and held hands and repeated the Lord's Prayer together. Then we left. It was maybe the first time I had ever been with a group of people who were all so terribly honest. There is a terribleness with that kind of honesty. There is also a power. I think that is the way it must have been when people hung out with Jesus. He would have been a tough one to be fake around. People knew he spoke the truth, but I am also pretty sure that truth emanated from him like a force field. If people came close enough to hear his voice they were close enough to lose their pretense, like someone shedding a bathrobe on the way to the shower.

That evening I was the only person who was hiding. I was just there to observe, not to participate. This is something Jesus never allowed. Around him you were participating whether you intended to or not. I walked out of the AA meeting feeling like I had been standing in truth that blazed like a furnace. It made me think of Shadrach, Meschak, and Abednego with the fourth person looking like a "son of God."[11] Jesus would have been at home in the bingo parlor that night. In fact I am pretty sure he was there. Later I blogged about it. Every time I mention I have a blog I am reminded of a T-shirt I saw. It said, "More people have read my T-shirt than have read your blog." That is undoubtedly true of my blog, but Tim Elliott read it and then wrote this email:

Hi, my name is Tim, I'm an alcoholic. Stating the truth of who I am has changed the answer to the question of why I'm here on this planet. Today I know who I am and what my purpose is. I went to my first 12-Step meeting in 1981. I was a lost and broken younger man. I was not looking to be accepted. I was not looking for a spiritual solution to my problems. I was angry and desperate with no other place to go. Jesus does hang out at 12-Step meetings, always has. It's why I love this fellowship and still go weekly. I see the evidence of God every time I go.

I first met "Jesus" at a 12-Step meeting in Chagrin Falls in 1982. Her name was Dotti. She was about fifty, thin, tall, big hair and big glasses (it was the 80s) and weathered by the bottle. She would stand at the exit and say goodnight to folks on their way out. Every week she would hug me and say, "Timothy! You are loved in a very special way!" I thought, *Whatever, you are a freak. Just give me a hug and leave me alone.* She did this for a year. Week after week. She never stopped. She never gave up. I wondered why. Every Tuesday, "Timothy! You are loved in a very special way!" Finally I had to ask her. "Dotti," I said, "What do you mean? What is this special way I am loved?" She told me the Creator of everything loved me. *Freak*, I thought. "What do you mean?" I asked. She told me that I had been looking for God all my life. That I had looked in some really bad places and did not find him. She told me that God was looking for me too, for a really long time, like all my life and before. *Freak*. That

He wants to know me and He wants me to know him. She told me I belonged to him . . . that I was His. Dotti looked into my soul and told me who I was and why I was here. I could tell she wasn't lying. I could see it in her eyes.

A few weeks later I opened a Bible for the first time and read the truth. It made sense . . . slowly. I learned of the problem, the symptoms, and the solution.

Hi, my name is Tim. I'm a liar, luster, idolater, thief, phony churchgoer, judge of others, proud, manipulator, fornicator, breaker of the law, selfish, self-centered, arrogant, sought, found, bought by Him.

In Christ,

Tim

⌒

Years ago I remember reading a story about the famous evangelist Harry Ironsides. The Salvation Army was holding an outdoor meeting and the speaker noticed Dr. Ironsides in the crowd. He invited him up on the makeshift stage. As Dr. Ironsides made his way up, a heckler who was known to be an outspoken atheist began to yell and challenge Dr. Ironsides to a debate. Dr. Ironsides stood there a moment thinking. Finally he said, "Yes, I will debate you this Saturday morning. But there is one condition. You bring one person whose life has been transformed by the power of becoming an atheist and I will bring fifty ex-alcoholics and fifty ex-prostitutes whose lives have been transformed by the power of Jesus Christ. And then we will debate." There was no debate. The heckler hoped to stay in the realm of words and ideas. Dr. Ironsides dragged the debate into real life. Or better, Ironsides was going to put real lives on display, lives that had been dragged into the light of truth, stripped naked, and clothed again with a truth deeper still. The one thing that has always made being naked seem okay is love. It is the only way anyone has ever been able to handle truth. Harry Ironsides decided the debate should have both truth and love in abundance, so even before it started he set the cross dead center.

Jack Nicholson yelled the famous line, "You can't handle the truth." He was right. There are very few who can. But whenever it happens you can be sure that Jesus is not far away.

BOB

Maybe you didn't notice, but Joe had to resort to telling other peoples' stories in this chapter about lying. In my section, you won't hear about anybody's lies but my own. You see, I'm a natural-born liar. And that's the truth. As a mere fifth grader I won first place in the Lincoln Elementary School Tall Tale Contest. I'm not making that up. I actually got a trophy for it at the year-end awards ceremony.

The desire to enhance one's image is always fertile ground for lies. In tenth grade my friends threw a birthday party for me and got me a 12-pack of really cheap beer. I didn't want to puke, or worse yet, get in trouble with my dad. So every fifteen minutes I cracked open a beer, staggered into the bathroom, locked the door, poured it into the toilet, and flushed it down. Then I washed my hands and staggered out with the near-empty can. If you were there that night you thought I was plastered. But it was all an act. My image, however, was definitely enhanced.

At age sixteen I heard the gospel for the first time. When they got to the part where I was a sinner, I immediately agreed. By that point in my life I was keenly aware that my desire for perpetual image enhancement had turned me into a compulsive liar. I responded to the gospel immediately, and to my utter amazement, the lying stopped. It was effortless. That lasted for a couple years, I think, and then it gradually crept back in. It's as if the drive for enhancing my image had been woven into the fabric of my soul.

By my mid-thirties my first wife, Rita, had me pegged. She observed that I became like whomever I was around. When I was around Scotch-drinking, cigar-smoking businessmen, I drank Scotch and smoked cigars. I dressed and talked and acted just like them. But when I was around Christians, I spoke their language and fit right in with their do's and don'ts. She came up with a nickname for me: *Chameleon*. It was hardly a term of endearment. I hated that nickname. But it was a perfect fit and we both knew it.

⌒

I've been dreading this next part of my story. Not because I'm afraid to publicly admit what I did. I've been open about it for over a decade. I'm dreading it because Rita and our kids, Dave and Lauren, will eventually read this and re-experience the pain of being hacked to pieces by my sin. They will understand my purpose for sharing this with you. But it still hurts and I'm really sorry for that.

Joe wrote that lies are like webs that wrap around us and bind us. By the time I hit forty, I was wrapped up like a mummy. But there's something about lies Joe did not tell you. Lies move you even while they bind you. They don't move you the way stepping-stones move you. With stepping-stones you're the one in control. Lies have a power to make you move. The bigger the lie, the greater the movement. And a pack of lies has more power than a single one. Every lie moves you in a common direction—they force you farther away from truth and reality.

Lies are like waves pushing driftwood toward the shore. People who get entangled in major deceptions like extramarital affairs learn to surf lies. It's a balancing act to stay above water. One wave breaks and there's another one right behind it. And another. And another. They are relentless. A simple question like, "Where were you this afternoon?" can cause you to surf four or five lies before you hang up your coat. Not long after my affair with Amy started I began lying about nearly everything. I was even lying about my lying. Each lie moved me a little bit further from the person I was once crazy about.

The lies you *tell* have power to move you an inch at a time. But the lies you *believe* make you lunge forward with a force that can take your breath away. In my case there were two such lies. The first was a simple, common lie: "I deserve better." The second was even more compelling because it contained a subtle half-truth: "God just wants me to be happy." Over the course of the next few months those two lies would grow and then combine into a tidal wave that would utterly drown the voice of my conscience.

Before long most of my family and friends were riding the waves with me. I heard their affirmations: "You deserve to be happy." "Just follow your heart." "You gotta do what's right for you." I don't put any blame on them for what I did. Their words were just echoing the lies I had already bought into.

Surfers are exhilarated by the kind of wave that forms a tube they can ride in. One day I found myself believing a new lie and it instantly became my ultimate tube wave. It swallowed up all my other waves and rationalizations: "My kids need a model of a healthy marriage—this is best for my kids." I was now flying through the tube. I knew the tipping point was inevitable, so instead of waiting to be caught, I dove in headfirst. The water was frigid but I was already numb. I hired a lawyer, bought a vacant two-bedroom condo with a loft, and called a moving company.

I moved out of the house that had been Rita's dream home. I did it while she was skiing in Idaho with Lauren and Dave. They were nine and ten years old. When they came home all my stuff had been cleared out and half the furniture was missing.

A month later, Amy left her husband and moved into the condo. We set up the spare bedroom for her and told the kids she was my roommate. I think they actually believed us, or at least they wanted to.

It seemed like my plan was working, but Amy and I struggled to adjust to living together. The beach we had washed up on was no tropical paradise. It was covered with sharp rocks and poisonous jellyfish and piles of reeking trash. After living together for less than two weeks, I came home from work and all Amy's stuff was gone. When I saw the fist-size hole in the wall, I knew she was back with her husband. It was Easter week, 1996. I walked around the condo shell-shocked and sick to my stomach. Want to know how out of touch with reality I was? How wrapped up in my own selfish schemes? It took years for me to realize that this must have been something like the way Rita, Dave, and Lauren had felt when they returned from Idaho. Except their pain was undoubtedly far worse than mine.

A couple weeks later I was standing in the loft looking down from the balcony, alone. More alone, really, than could be explained by Amy's absence. I suddenly realized I no longer had any awareness of God's love. None. I remember desperately trying to remember, and I couldn't. I was drowning, and there was nothing real to grab hold of to keep me afloat.

Amy's attempt to reconcile with her husband was short-lived. She moved back to the condo on the Fourth of July and her marriage was "dissolved" around Labor Day. But something in her had changed and we both knew it. She was bound and determined never to lie again. Ever. It was like she developed an allergy to lying the way some people become allergic to peanuts. As though if she lied again she would die. She's been that way to this day. But it didn't soothe her conscience one bit.

She soon told me she was overwhelmed with guilt, and that she needed to go to church. She was Roman Catholic so that's where she wanted to go. I had my doubts but I took her anyway. Each Sunday on the way home I would fill her in on what the Bible said about the various aspects of the Mass we'd heard. I had memorized hundreds of Scripture verses during my early days at Ohio State, and in spite of the fact that I hadn't picked up a Bible in eight years I still retained a lot of it. But Amy didn't believe me. By the third Sunday she had had enough, "You and I are going to read the Bible." So we did. Every day.

We read through the New Testament a couple chapters at a time. Amy had never read the Bible before so everything was new and fresh and wondrous. She was especially struck every time Jesus started out by saying, "Truly, truly I say to you . . ." To me, every verse felt like a drop of clean, cool water on the tongue of a man dying of thirst. *Why did I ever walk away from this?*

One day it hit me. I was alone again in the loft looking down from the balcony when I saw it: his love and grace and mercy all run together in a single channel that flows red. Like blood. And in that instant of time, I knew for sure that he loved me. In spite of all I had done and how far I had fallen.

⌒

I wish I could say the rest of the story was warm and fuzzy, but to be honest, it was just the opposite. Life was a mess. To say my relationship with Amy was unstable would be an understatement. Meanwhile, Dave and Lauren did their best to adjust to their fractured family life. I'm proud of them for that. As Christmas approached, Rita's life was shattered a second time—she was diagnosed with stage IV breast cancer. That meant chemotherapy and radical mastectomy. She lost her hair and even her eyebrows. She was always pretty, and still is. I hope someday you can read the book she is writing about her journey. If you do you will be inspired.

Amy and I became painfully aware that several people who had watched us riding our now abandoned lies were surfing very similar lies with gusto. One of them was my younger sister. I decided to confront her, to warn her not to go there. She looked me in the eye and said, "It worked for you." I became frantic and before long I was screaming at the top of my lungs, "NO! It didn't." I literally shook her, but no matter what I said or did, she wouldn't listen. More and more friends joined the surf party. There were separations and divorces left and right. The example of my life could not be undone. As I helplessly watched the wave ripple through the lives of those around me, I realized it would eventually wash over generations yet unborn—Dave's kids, Lauren's kids, and more.

Amy and I got married the weekend after my divorce was final. It was July 18, 1997. One picture from the wedding is permanently etched on my mind: The look in Dave's eyes as he struggled to smile. Fourteen years have passed since then, and the memory still causes me to wince. "Time heals all wounds" is a lie you can ride right into a full-blown depression.

When you believe a lie it's like swallowing little bits of glass, and when you tell a lie it's like feeding them to those who hear. The damage happens internally, so it's hard to detect at first. The ultimate effects may not show up until years later. I've watched this in my kids. I don't completely understand it, but I know it's true. I can feel it in my stomach. And I can see it in their eyes. The glass is still down there from years ago. Even though, years ago, the Savior cut the webs that bound me.

By now it will probably make sense when I tell you that the person in the Bible I identify with the most is the sinful woman in Luke 7:36-50. She was an immoral person, probably a prostitute. She had an initial encounter with Jesus that we're not told about, but it's safe to assume he had offered her forgiveness. When she discovered she could see him a second time she ran home, got the most expensive thing she owned, an alabaster flask of ointment worth thousands, and then ran to the home of Simon the Pharisee where Jesus was dining. She arrived with a plan to anoint the Lord's feet. But before she could get the flask open, she had a spontaneous outburst of affection. She began to weep. She wet his feet with her tears and wiped them with her long hair. And she kissed his feet.

When Simon discredited Jesus for allowing himself to be touched like this by such an unclean person, Jesus told a story about a moneylender who had two debtors. One owed ten times more than the other. When neither could repay him, the moneylender canceled the debts of both. Jesus turned to Simon and asked, "Which of the two will love him more?" Simon got the point, "The one, I suppose, for whom he canceled the larger debt." Jesus smiled at the woman and agreed.

But Jesus didn't stop there. He wasn't just tolerating this woman. He turned to her and publicly declared, "Your sins are forgiven . . . your faith has saved you; go in peace." This was no empty declaration, either. Jesus knew he was heading to the cross to personally pay that woman's debt in full, to purchase with his shed blood the grace he had just given her so freely.

I think I know how the sinful woman felt on that remarkable day. She couldn't help herself. Her tears flowed from overwhelming gratitude. She thought, *How can it be? I don't deserve forgiveness. Not at all.*

I'm right there with her. A mountain of sin requires a mountain of forgiveness. Of course she and I love much. How could we not?

But my love for Jesus is far from perfect. Truth is, I don't love him nearly enough. Not even close. If precious ointment were love there couldn't be enough on the planet to offer him the love he deserves. And yet I can *only* love him, even a little, because he decided to love me first.[12] His love for me is there in the pages of Scripture, in the story of the gospel, news so good it seems too good to be true. And yet it is the most solid reality and the most profound truth in the universe.

And what does this good news of the gospel have to do with Rita and Lauren and Dave? Good question. It's fourteen years later, and I tell you the truth, we've seen some amazing magic in our family. Call it healing. Complete in some places, partial in others. But not because time heals all wounds. Something much deeper is going on. Something connected to grace, and mercy, and love that flows red like blood. That story continues in chapter 13.

6

Independence
and a Toothpick Cross

JOE

Someone sent me a link to a YouTube video called the "Milk Jug God." It was a monologue from a fairly bright, fairly sarcastic young atheist. He was praying to a jug of milk. He claimed that the milk jug could pretty much equal the Christian God when it came to answering prayer. His Christian friends had defended prayer by saying God always answers, but the answer can be one of three possibilities. God may say Yes, and the request is granted; No, and the request denied; or (and this is the great escape valve) Maybe, and the request is put on the divine backburner for an indefinite time. The YouTube atheist made the same claim for the milk jug. Of course, he was right. Yes, No, or Maybe are the only answers to any request. But applying it to God and wrapping it in a thick layer of sarcasm was pretty effective.

Doubt hits me like a sniper. I hardly ever see it coming. Once when I took my family to Disney World we went to a Christian amusement park called The Holy Land Experience. Amusement parks are something Christians should avoid developing. We are just not very good at amusing people and that is okay. But setting people up to be amused and preaching at them instead is probably a sin or at least it should be. I have friends who went to Israel and came back with their faith on fire. I was hoping this park would at least set me smoldering a little, and who knows what it could do for my kids who were recovering from Disney overload.

There was a big room set up as a miniature Jerusalem. It reminded me of how grown men can get carried away with toy soldiers and end up re-creating Gettysburg in their basement. As the guide pointed a penlight to the different sites I became more and more uncomfortable. There was Pilate's palace the size of a thimble. The house of Caiaphas stood close by along with the small house where the disciples shared the Last Supper with Jesus. The penlight finally swung outside the city gates to a tiny hill. On top of the hill stood three crosses made of toothpicks. Right then the sniper fired. I thought, "So, this is what I am basing my life on. That a single man was put to death on a toothpick cross in the middle of a tiny country somewhere in the middle of a tiny planet somewhere in the middle of a tiny galaxy." A milk-jug god.

My friend Andrew is a lawyer. He is very bright and grew up as an atheist. He wasn't just an atheist by default. He had really thought it through. He was convinced to the point of being smug, meaning he thought anyone who was not an atheist was just silly. I think that cracks God up.[13] It would me if I were God. After law school Andrew got a clerking job for a federal judge. The judge was a brilliant woman who had graduated first in her class from law school. Andrew says she is one of the smartest people he has ever known which is why he remembers where he was standing the first time he heard her say that Jesus was her Lord and Savior. Andrew was stunned. He had no idea someone so brilliant could be so silly.

When Andrew was in high school he read a book by Richard Bach called *Illusions: The Adventures of a Reluctant Messiah.* The book is filled with pithy sayings intended to help people become self-actualized. Andrew gleaned his purpose in life from one of the pages of the book. He decided his purpose is to learn and have fun. This gave him both moral freedom and intellectual superiority, which when you think about it is a pretty awesome philosophical system. After that day when the judge mentioned Jesus, Andrew waited a couple of days and then decided to share his wisdom with her. He walked into her office and said, "Judge, I know what my purpose in life is." She said, "Really, that's great Andrew. What is it?" With great confidence and a glaze of smugness he answered, "The purpose of my life is to learn and have fun." He fully expected to stun her out of her silliness. Instead she looked up at him with her steely blue eyes and said, "Andrew, that is the stupidest thing I ever heard."

Until I met Andrew I never knew that doubt plagued atheists too. You have to admit it was unorthodox evangelism but that comment by the judge was strong enough to wound Andrew. He spent the next few months bleeding out.

After clerking, Andrew landed a dream job with a prestigious firm in the city. His arrogance ended up costing him that job. He got winged a couple more times before he and his wife crawled into our church. An atheist really has nowhere to go, and doubt was dragging Andrew down like wolves drag down a deer. To be an atheist requires independence that borders on the heroic. I say heroic because a human being can only exist several weeks without food, several days without water, and several minutes without air. To simply survive moment by moment we need for dozens of invisible things to keep on happening as reliably as the sunrise. We also have social needs that must be met or we start to get strange. Human beings are about as dependent as a creature can possibly be. Feigning independence takes an enormous amount of energy and chutzpah. The other problem with declaring independence is that it's a sure way to remain alone forever.

⸻

My dad recently had a serious stroke. He and my mom have been married for fifty-two years. Mom and I sat in the hospital emergency room waiting for a doctor to come and tell us how much of my dad we would cart out of the hospital. A stroke takes a whole person and subtracts, which means the more severe the stroke the smaller the fraction that is left. At one point my mom turned to me and said, "I will take care of him you know. Whatever happens I will spend my life taking care of him. After the way he has taken care of me the last fifty years it is the least I can do. I mean it." My mom was making a declaration of love and it was about as far away from independence as one can get. Such is the nature of love. There is no real human love without need.

I was in Romania one time and visited a state-run orphanage in a town called Tinka. The facility had far too few workers to effectively care for the five hundred orphans living there. During one part of the tour we passed by a room of about fifty children who looked to be about five years old. When they saw us they broke out of their room and ran to us. They were all begging to be picked up. We each had a swarm of children around us begging, reaching up their skinny little arms and groaning. These were not children who were smiling and wanting to play. These were children who were so desperate for human affection they were grunting and whining like animals. I watched as one of my friends hoisted one of the children into his arms. The child clung wide-eyed to his neck. When he started to put the child down to pick up another, the first child screamed like he was being burned. We walked out of the orphanage an hour later in silence. No one knew what to say.

Human beings cannot survive without love. If independence was all those children needed they would have been the most well-adjusted people on the planet. Instead they had been reduced to something that honestly looked less than human.

⁓

Like I said, doubt shoots at me like an assassin. But after that theme park it didn't take me long to figure out why I believe in a God who would die on a toothpick cross in the middle of nowhere. Dependent beings must have a god. Carl Sagan mimicked the Gospel of John every time he opened his show by saying, "The cosmos is all there is, all there ever was, and all there ever will be."[14] And he was fond of saying we should thank our lucky stars because that is where we came from . . . literally. Sagan recognized that dependent beings have a need to offer thanks.

The Big Bang does all kinds of damage to the lucky-stars deity. So does entropy. But that is for another book and a smarter author. All I'm saying here is that we need more than a god who will supply us with air and food and water. We are the desperate orphans of Tinka. We are desperate for love. This is something a milk-jug god cannot give. It is something my lucky stars cannot provide. But a god who will come down and die on a toothpick cross in the middle of an obscure town, in the middle of an obscure country, in the middle of an obscure planet, in the middle of an obscure galaxy is exactly the kind of God I need. It was what my friend Andrew found when he crawled into our church. It has created in him a joy and a love that makes him one of my favorite people now.

Doubt shoots at me like an assassin. That is true enough. But the toothpick cross has become something that reminds me of Tinka. It reminds me of my own desperation. It reminds me of a God who did not forget that my greatest need is love.

BOB

I love music, pretty much all kinds. But I was raised on rock-n-roll. And while I'm no groupie, I have been up close and personal with several rock stars. I could tell you stories about my experiences with Tom Petty, Neil Young, and *The Who*'s Pete Townsend. But I'll stick to stories that help make my point.

Like this one. I got Paul McCartney to wink at my wife.

Amy and I had front row seats. About halfway through the concert I realized I was making eye contact with Paul about every two minutes. I started wracking my brain for a way to get interactive with him somehow. Then it hit me. The next time he looked right at me I pointed to Amy and motioned for him to blow her a kiss. Paul, good friend that he instantly became, not only blew her a kiss, he gave her one of his famous winks. That McCartney. He's always over the top. But here's my question. Why did he do it? He didn't do it because I am so clever and persuasive. He did it because that happened to be what he wanted to do at that moment.

You could make a case that rock stars are the most independent people on the planet. They spend their time doing exactly what they feel like doing—on tour or off. They sleep when they want. They eat whatever they want whenever they want and drink whatever they want whenever they want. Not to mention sex and drugs, but we don't need to go there.

I went to a Bruce Springsteen concert in 1985. As soon as the first encore started I left my relatively good seat and maneuvered all the way down to front row dead center. Don't ask me how. I just had a knack for it. A combination of patience, timing and stealth. From my new vantage point I basked in two more encores. As the band headed offstage waving goodbye, I blurted out, "Play 'Born to Run.' " Bruce turned around and looked right at me. I smiled with contentment as the fans screamed their lungs out. We were headed for a fourth encore and it would definitely be "Born to Run." I hope you play it as you read what happened next so you get the full effect. If you never heard of Springsteen, now's your chance. Oh, and be sure to Google the lyrics.

I couldn't wait for the saxophone solo halfway through. It's my favorite part. And when it came, wouldn't you know it, the legendary Clarence Clemons walked up to me in the spotlight, looked me in the eye, put the bell of his sax square in my face, and wailed away. Just when I thought it couldn't get any better, it happened. The Boss walked right up to me and held his famous '50s Fender Esquire guitar directly over my head. I reached up and put my fingers on the strings. I pressed down. Bruce strummed. I randomly moved my fingers. I looked up at Bruce. Our eyes locked. Both of us could clearly hear the noise we were making. The other twenty-five thousand people were probably clueless about it because the band drowned us out. But Bruce and I shared a knowing grin as we collaborated on our lengthy guitar interlude. It was a moment at least one of us will always remember. But here's my point. Why did Bruce do this? He's a rock star—he did it because he wanted to. Not because I was the guy who yelled out, "Play 'Born to Run!' "

Independence is doing what you want, when you want, because you want to. Sounds good, doesn't it? All of us are wired for that. We are all wannabe rock stars. Especially me.

But there's something ironic about rock stars. With all their wealth and fame and ability to do whatever they want, they are pretty much a lock to develop an addiction. And what is an addiction? It's a *dependency*. The exact opposite of independence!

Why do rock stars get addicted? I remember how Joe put it one time—it's because "reality beats the crap out of independence." Rock stars are proof that independence can be a lot of fun, but rock star addictions are proof that independence is a mirage. It eventually disintegrates. Sometimes it vanishes gradually like ice. Other times it snaps like a firecracker.

⌒

Amy gave birth to a baby girl three days before Y2K. We named her Grace. Her name stood for everything good we knew in this world: *God's blessings through Christ toward those who deserve his curse.* Baby Grace arrived healthy, beautiful, and content. Wonder filled our hearts. The magic multiplied as Lauren and Dave bonded with her in the hospital. Grace brought a ray of hope that we would somehow end up like the blended families you read about sometimes. All was warm. All was fuzzy. Like Christmas when you still believed in Santa Claus.

Two months later, Grace broke out in a rash that looked like little dots. Amy called the pediatrician's office and was told not to worry about it; no need to bring her in, they said. Besides, they were busy with flu season. The next day the rash covered her tiny body and the dots were the size of pencil erasers. This time when we called they told us to rush her to the hospital. One drop of blood was all it took to diagnose the problem. Idiopathic thrombocytopenia. That meant Grace was not forming platelets, which meant her blood could not clot. It was not a rash at all. The spots were actually bruises caused by normal blood pressure. Internal bleeding in her little organs was inevitable. They did an ultrasound and discovered a brain hemorrhage. They told us Grace was dying. She had maybe forty-eight hours to live but we'd already wasted a day. In an instant of time, reality snapped every shred of independence and replaced it with a desperate sense of dependence.

They moved Grace to the hematology ward where all the other kids were bald because they had leukemia. Amy choked back tears whenever she'd see one of them, but to me it seemed like they were always smiling. We were told there was only one hope for Grace, several hours hooked up to a plastic bag filled with a dark brown juice called immunoglobulin G. The nurse shook her head and sighed, "All we can do now is wait and pray." We already knew that. Amy wept silently as I got on the telephone to call in some prayer from the nice folks at Church in the Valley. If ever there was a time to kick in their Prayer Chain, it was now. Meanwhile, with the juice dripping into her body, Grace was as sweet and content as any two-month-old you have ever known.

When the bag was empty they took a drop of blood. No platelets. Amy wailed uncontrollably. They hooked up another bag. With a lump in my throat the size of a tennis ball I asked, "If the first bag didn't work, what makes you think this one will?" "All we can do is try." Six hours later, no platelets. We prepared to say goodbye to little Grace.

Amy and I prayed as the seconds ticked away like a sledgehammer on a steel anvil. There was no mention of doctors in these prayers. We were now dependent on God alone. We felt totally, and I mean totally, helpless. Joe said doubt comes at him out of the blue, like a sniper scoping him out at 200 yards. But I saw doubt coming like a freight train a half-mile away and there was nothing I could do to stop it. I sat holding our little girl in my arms and doubt marched into the room and completely commandeered my thoughts. "What is God doing?" doubt snickered at me, "Does he even care about this child?"

But Grace was still breathing, so we kept praying. When you stop and think about it, *every* prayer is an expression of dependency on God.

The senior pediatric hematologist arrived with another bag of juice. This one was as black as night. He had an idea. "These are live human platelets. It's not a recognized treatment, but if you sign here I'll infuse them." Amy wiped her tears with her sleeve and signed with her eyes closed.

Grace was released from the hospital the next day. Her platelet count shot up to normal and has never looked back. I brought the car around, we strapped the car seat in and everyone but Grace cried all the way home.

That Sunday in church I held Grace as we got up to thank the small congregation of people for praying. Before I was done, an older lady stood up. She was not one of my favorites because she was always stiff and stuffy. She said, "There were over two thousand people praying for Grace." It turns out that her prayer chain kicked in two other big prayer chains, which kicked in a half dozen others. It was a chain reaction of prayer. Two thousand people expressing dependency on God in unison. After the service I hugged that lady. We later made another startling discovery—even Rita had been praying for Grace.

Idiopathic thrombocytopenia had been a crash course in depending on God. In the process he drew me close. I got up before the sun on Monday morning to check on Grace. No spots and her breath was sweet. As I watched her sleep in the early morning stillness, I had a conversation with God. I told him how silly my perceived independence had been. I'd been taught from an early age that independence was a solid virtue, but it turned out to be a wispy illusion. In my hour of desperate need, my mirage disappeared right there in Children's Hospital. I thanked him for that. I admitted that I am totally dependent on him. Always have been. Always will be.

That's when I realized I'd always been dependent—but on all the wrong things. Money. Control. Business success. Personal accomplishments. Good health. Family. But none of these could save Grace. None of them could save me. When real need arises, they all fall down. That's when the truth hit me—dependence, being focused on the living God alone, is what I was made for.

I opened the Bible and God drew me closer yet. He spoke from his Word so clearly it startled me. "Whatever the Lord pleases, he does, in heaven and on earth, in the seas and all deeps."[15] The pieces of the epiphany were coming together. I responded, *You do what you want when you want—that makes you the only Person in the entire universe who is truly independent. And your absolute independence is precisely the reason I can absolutely depend on you.*

I was having a cathartic experience as he pointed to the cross-reference:

The God who made the world and everything in it, being Lord of heaven and earth, does not live in temples made by man, nor is he served by human hands, as though he needed anything, since he himself gives to all mankind life and breath and everything.[16]

You have no needs. You are dependent on no one. Yet I'm dependent on you for the very breath I breathe, for the breath Grace breathes. Seeing my dependence in the light of his independence took me to a place I'd never been before—to an overwhelming sense of calm. And suddenly I no longer had a desire to be a rock star.

But the best part of the morning was yet to come. With my fresh understanding of God's independence, where do you think he took me next? To my toothpick cross.

> I am the good shepherd. The good shepherd lays down his life for the sheep.... No one takes it from me, but I lay it down of my own accord. I have authority to lay it down, and I have authority to take it up again.[17]

I could barely breathe as I responded to my Shepherd,.

Jesus, you voluntarily left your independence behind so you could lay down your life for me, a silly sheep.

A favorite passage thundered into my mind and I formed the words into a prayer:[18]

Jesus, though you were in the form of the absolutely independent God, you didn't count your equality with God a thing to be grasped, but you made yourself nothing, taking the form of a servant, being born in the likeness of men. And being found in human form, you humbled yourself by becoming obedient to the point of death, even death on a cross.

For the first time I realized Jesus didn't do this because God had some kind of need. There could only be one reason. He did it for the love of his sheep.

What did I doubt at Children's Hospital? I doubted his love. My guess is similar doubts have hit you as well. Right now the cross might seem to you about as big as a couple of toothpicks. I know the feeling. But get in the shadow of that cross, even that tiny one, and you'll get a glimpse of God's love and find the power to move doubt back to faith.

You may think that's easy for me to say since my little Grace got better. But now I know there's a God who loves me, a God who did not withhold his only Child from me. And that Child grew up and laid down his life for me. Because of the cross I know that God's love remains the same, even if Grace dies in our arms someday.

7

Carrots, Money and the Giant Within

JOE

A lot of people think God talks to them. I think a lot of people are wrong. But every once in a while someone will tell me something God said to them and it really sounds like God.

Gene, my charismatic friend, told me he was on a kick where he was in constant communion with God. He had read an obscure passage in Isaiah that said, "And your ears shall hear a word behind you, saying, 'This is the way, walk in it,' when you turn to the right or when you turn to the left."[19] After reading that passage he decided he would trust God for direction in every area of his life. He even quit carrying maps in his car, and this was before GPS. One time he was out in the country and had forgotten the directions to where he was going. He sat at a stop sign and prayed. He felt compelled to go left. He turned left and about a mile down the road it became evident this was the wrong direction. Gene told me it really shook him up. He pulled off the road and beseeched heaven. "God, I don't understand. I asked for direction and I felt you said to go left and it was wrong. What is going on?" Gene leaned close to me and said in complete earnestness, "Joe, as clearly as God has ever spoken to me he said, 'Gene, quit asking me stupid questions.' " I think Gene heard from the living God.

My friend Frank is dead serious about God. He is intense. I love the way Frank talks about God. He talks about God like he is in the room and wildly dangerous. Whenever I talk to Frank about God I feel like a telephone pole has just fallen down near me and wires are whipping around like electric snakes and a single wrong move could kill me. I like talking to Frank about God. I was talking to Frank the other day and he told me he had had his first vision. *Wild*, I thought, *this is going to be too cool.*

Frank said that in his vision he woke up in the morning and there was a plant on his head. It wasn't exactly on his head; it was growing out of his head. He could reach up and feel it. It was a tangle of vines. He looked down at his leg and could see that the vine root went down through his right leg. It was a huge root that came to an end at the bottom of his foot. He could feel this vine was killing him. It was like human kudzu. Then he felt God reach down and grab the tangle of vines on his head and pull. God pulled the whole thing out of him like a farmer would pull a huge carrot out of the ground. Frank looked at me with his dead serious eyes. Electric wires snapped around the room. Frank said, "Joe, do you know what the plant was?" "No," I said, keeping my eyes peeled for God. I wanted to make it out of Frank's living room alive. "It was pride," Frank said. God had pulled pride out of Frank like a carrot. Then Frank said, "It felt awesome. I felt amazing for a minute. Then I looked down through the hollow thigh to my right foot. And do you know what I saw? I saw a tiny vine already starting to grow right where God had ripped the root out. It wasn't five seconds, and pride was already growing back." Frank is bona fide.

Pride is relentless. It feeds on virtually anything. I'm told one of my staff members brushes his teeth five times a day. I chuckle to myself and the vine of pride grows. Tell me anything about yourself and I can turn it to feed the pride that lives inside me. I heard about a pastor who recognized his problem of pride. To humble himself he decided to volunteer at the local soup kitchen mopping floors. Swabbing the floor in the middle of the night he caught himself thinking, "I have got to be the only pastor in this whole city who is humble enough to do this." I understand that guy.

Pride isn't just exaggerating stories or accomplishments. Pride is an inflation of the soul. It is an exaggeration of my very being. It is sinister, it is relentless, it is crippling. There is only one thing in the universe strong enough to actually haul pride out by the roots.

Soon after my wife and I married we moved to Florida. We lived in a tiny house in a new subdivision. We had just enough money to landscape the front yard. The back yard was au natural. Florida is a beautiful place mainly because of modern irrigation. Most of the state is sand and my back yard was no exception. Someone had given us a refrigerator and I borrowed a van to pick it up. It was my day off and I was feeling young and virile which is a pretty deadly combination. I decided if I could get the van close enough to my kitchen I would be able to wrestle the refrigerator into the house by myself. I pulled around to the back of the house to unload the fridge. I don't want to brag but that afternoon I completely dominated the appliance world. Everything went like I thought it would. It was right on the edge of being stupid but my youthful strength overcame stupid and I headed back out to the van sweaty, smug, and satisfied, the refrigerator humming away inside. As I started to pull the van out of the yard I felt the tires spin.

We had moved to Florida from the Snow Belt so I was far from panicking at first. I got out of the van and took a look at the problem. The van sat on a fairly large patch of sand and the rear tires had sunk a couple of inches. I grabbed some debris that was lying around and put it under one of the tires for traction. The next time I got out of the van the rear tires were beginning to disappear. The Florida sun was beating down and I was now covered with sweat and grit. I did everything I could think of. Nothing worked. The van was hopelessly stuck and there was nothing more for me to do.

I was standing surveying the damage when my neighbor called over from the edge of his yard. "Hey Joe, do you need some help?" He looked mildly amused. I wondered how long he had been watching. It could hardly have been more obvious that I needed help. I probably needed help the minute I made the decision to wrestle a major appliance. I feigned a smile and said, "Thanks Stan, but I'm good. I think I'll be okay." He came over five minutes later with his pickup truck, tied a chain onto the bumper of the van, and pulled me out.

Now, here is the question. Why would I refuse help when I knew I needed it so desperately? Because during the whole ordeal my pride had been taking a beating, yet it was still alive and well right up until the very end. When my neighbor offered help, to me he was just offering death. My refusal was an attempt to keep my pride alive even if it had shriveled to a tiny sprig. He was not just asking me if I needed help, he was asking me if I needed a savior. The only person who really needs a savior is someone who is helpless and hopeless. The only thing that will make me admit my need for a savior is if I am convinced I am both helpless and hopeless. If my neighbor had charged me $20 for the tow then I still could have salvaged some pride. But to pull me out for nothing, that was just downright ruthless. I had nothing to give but gratitude.

As I stood with Stan in my back yard and thanked him, I was small but solid. I had been reduced to the real size of my soul. I spend so little time that size it always feels smaller than it should. It was grace Stan gave me and grace is kryptonite to pride. It is the only element the world has ever known that effectively takes pride by the root and pulls it out.

C. S. Lewis walked into a room where some of his friends had been having a discussion for several hours. He asked what they were talking about. They said, "We have been discussing what makes Christianity different than all other religions." C. S. Lewis said, "That's easy. It's grace." And he walked out of the room. He was right. A single word captures the difference between Christianity and all other religions. Grace.

Every other religion allows me to pay at least something for the tow. And if I pay anything at all then pride will wolf it down and the vines will begin to grow with a terrible ferocity. All my pride needs is credit for a single good thing. If I can take credit for seeking God then my pride lives. But Christianity allows nothing of the sort. It is the shepherd who seeks the sheep. It is the sheep who is lost and hopeless and helpless. So it is the cross or it is nothing at all. That is why the cross is death before it is life. Even with Jesus it was the cross and only then the resurrection. Grace makes it the same for us.

If it is true that pride is inflation of the soul then the only time we are the size of our true self is when we are devoid of pride. Grace is the only thing in all the universe with the power to destroy the pride that grows so relentlessly in my soul.

In Frank's vision, God reached down and pulled pride out of him like a giant carrot. Frank told me it was the only time he ever felt really free. The only thing that gets Frank more jazzed than talking about God is when he talks about the cross. It is the cross that made Frank real, and it is grace that grabbed his head and changed his soul that day.

BOB

Several years ago I had a sense of déjà vu while reading 1 Peter 5:5. *God is opposed to the proud.* I clicked on the cross-reference and realized James 4:6 says exactly the same thing. Word for word. The repetition got my attention and I paused long enough to let the truth of the twin verses sink in. God stands in active opposition to my pride. That was not good news. It shook me to the core. I don't want God to oppose me. Who does? I felt a need to take immediate action to do something about my pride. I didn't know how to change, so I did the next best thing. I bought a book on the subject. It was a little book called, *Humility: True Greatness,* by C. J. Mahaney. Here are three of the sentences I read in chapter 2:

> Pride is when sinful human beings aspire to the status and position of God and refuse to acknowledge their dependence on him.

> Pride not only appears to be the first sin, but it is at the core of all sin.

> There's no sin more offensive to God than pride.

I thought it over and came to the conclusion that God had really good reasons to oppose to my pride. I felt like I was going to barf.

Frank had that vision about vines, but for me pride is like a giant living inside me. I feed the giant every day and it grows. Sometimes I muster up the courage to do battle with it. I kick it in the shins and then run like hell. Every now and then I sling a stone at it from a distance, but I never hit it between the eyes. If I hit it at all, my stones ricochet off and drop to the ground like pebbles. And the giant never even blinks. When I undertake to engage pride in these ways, I always lose.

I think Joe did an excellent job discussing pride. He obviously knows a great deal about the subject. Joe comes by it honestly. In the first place, he's chisel-faced handsome with the body of an ironman. That gives pride an unfair advantage before Joe even gets out of bed. I actually overheard someone jokingly say, "Joe is too good looking for his own good." To make matters worse, people are always telling him what a gifted preacher he is, and how this or that message changed their lives. That's a dicey situation for a person who seeks to destroy pride.

But I've got news for Joe. When it comes to pride, he might as well face it—mine is bigger than his. And as you'll soon find out, Joe's pride is nowhere near as butt-ugly as mine. You're probably already convinced, but I'll explain just in case. There are many categories where I could shed light for you on the giant within me. But I'll stick to just one. Money.

I got my first job when I was sixteen. I scooped ice cream and mopped floors. The owner paid me a dollar an hour, which was less than minimum wage. I didn't care because I was still somewhat humble back then. I remained pretty much broke all through college. My net worth was about five hundred bucks the day Rita and I got married. But I also had my doctor of optometry degree from Ohio State (go Buckeyes) and a promising job working at a well-established practice. Not long after I started making an income I made two interesting discoveries. Money had a tremendous power to inflate my ego. And I liked that a lot.

Each year I made more and more. And I spent more and more in order to look like I had more than I really did. The day I drove home a two-seater sports car I looked like a millionaire, but I was not even close.

I enjoyed feeding the giant. He seemed like such a friendly, gentle giant. But he was getting fatter and uglier every day. We bought a house and sold it for a profit after three years. We bought another one, fixed it up, and made a killing on it five years later. Finally we bought Rita's dream home, an English Tudor built in the 1930s. It had a slate roof and a great big fireplace with a mantle made from carved stone. By this time my giant was bigger than me. Rita could see it. She pointed it out to me with sentences like, "You are an arrogant bastard and everyone at the office hates you." Rita doesn't mince words.

You can't blame her, she was absolutely right and I knew it. I even started to hate the giant a little. But it had taken on a life of its own. I had no clue how to do battle with it. I tried harder, exerting more willpower, and the giant giggled. I took sensitivity training and applied psychological insights. This time I heard belly laughs. I got the message. My self-improvement project was a joke. Meanwhile my giant was taking its toll on our marriage. And you already know how that turned out.

One would think a major breakdown like a failed marriage would produce a considerable amount of humility. But that's not how it went. The first year Amy and I were married I doubled my income by becoming a business development consultant on the side. A couple years later I co-founded a LASIK company. The year after Amy gave birth to Grace I made well over a million dollars. The next year I nearly doubled that amount. Prior to that, I was already an arrogant bastard. But my income from those two years launched me to the next level. Pompous ass. At least that's what Amy told me. Let me put it in a nutshell for you. I made a bunch of money and fed it to the giant. And my investment portfolio bloated its stomach causing a profound case of *flatulenza di orgoglio*. That's Italian for "flatulence of pride."

Money allows a person to buy a lot of giant food. I bought my dream home. It was totally unlike Rita's. It was a log cabin, but it was 7,500 square feet and looked like a Colorado ski lodge. I pointed out to my mom that the garage was bigger than the house I grew up in on Orrville Avenue. It had five cozy stone fireplaces, including one in the master bedroom. I told my mom the fireplaces alone were worth as much as the average home in Cuyahoga Falls and she seemed impressed.

I could tell you about other stuff I bought to feed the giant, but you already get the point. And I get why you're about ready to hurl. But hang in there, it gets worse.

A couple years after I bought the log cabin I decided I no longer enjoyed or wanted the "status" that came with it. Little by little my values were changing and eventually the whole concept of being a conspicuous consumer began to nauseate me. So I started divesting myself of the trappings of wealth. I gave a lot of money away. I opened my checkbook to the poor and blind and downtrodden. I even traded in my BMW for a pickup truck.

For a while it appeared that the giant was shrinking. But that was only an illusion. The giant in me merely changed clothes. I traded my material pride for something far worse—spiritual pride. Spiritual pride seems much healthier on the surface. It was as if I started feeding the giant huge amounts of organic fruits and vegetables. But if you've ever eaten too much raw broccoli, you know what happens. The *flatulenza* moves into the realm of the explosive.

People's reactions to me during this period were telling. When you're relatively rich and display your wealth through your possessions, sometimes people tend to hate you. That's understandable, so you just accept it. But when you throw in the towel on making money and start giving it away and relinquishing your expensive toys, you expect a little love. But I wasn't feeling the love. In retrospect it's not too surprising—people aren't stupid. They could see right through my false humility and self-serving generosity.

Joe pointed out that no matter what we do, pride is inside us gobbling up anything and everything. Big and small, good and bad, high and low, over and out. It's an inescapable, ever-present reality. I felt defeated by pride the day I bought C. J.'s book. The giant had brought me to my knees—but it turns out that's exactly where God wanted me. Humbled by my pride.

⌒

I thank God that C. J. did not end his little book at chapter 2. As I continued reading I realized I had been looking for hope in all the wrong places. On page 52, I read a single sentence that was worth the price of the book. "We cannot free ourselves from pride and selfish ambition; a divine rescue is absolutely necessary." I immediately agreed with the first part. Battling pride in my own strength is hopeless because the giant is too powerful for me. But it was the second part that gave me real hope. A divine rescue—Jesus and the cross. My eyes were opened. And the giant blinked for the first time.

There are two ways the cross rescues me from the grip of the giant. First, on the cross, Jesus delivered me from the *guilt* of sin—all the guilt, condemnation, and punishment I deserve for allowing the giant of sinful pride to live at the core of my soul. Second, on the cross Jesus rescued me from the *power* of sin. Paul put it like this, "For sin will have no dominion over you, since you are not under law but under grace".[20] That was huge! It meant that because of the cross, the giant can no longer control me. Jesus has toppled the giant within me.

But don't get me wrong. The giant is still down there. It's not dead. It can't condemn me or control me, but it's still present and active. Its appetite is more voracious than ever. I think it will be that way until I take my last breath. But I no longer wage war in my own strength. Instead, I remember the cross. His humility. The price he paid. I reach out for strength to battle the giant, and it comes, sometimes with tears. If I screw up and sin, I repent and remember the cross and the guilt of my pride vanishes.

I've discovered that reflecting on what happened at the cross can even generate the power to *hate* pride. The old hymn-writer, Isaac Watts, puts it better than I can:

> When I survey the wondrous cross
> On which the Prince of Glory died,
> My richest gain I count but loss
> And pour contempt on all my pride.

Nowadays I think of the giant as a phantom. After all, the basis for pride is an illusion. It's not solid. It's not real. I like the way John Stott put it. "All of us have inflated views of ourselves . . . until we have visited a place called Calvary. It is there, at the foot of the cross, that we shrink to our true size."[21]

God opposes the proud. That was devastating news to me. But I also noticed there was a flip side to the twin verses I mentioned at the beginning. God also "gives grace to the humble." Grace is what I really need in this life. It's what I really want. God promises to give it to the humble. The humility in me is the size of a peanut, but those twin verses got me motivated to pursue it. And so did Isaiah 66:1-2,

> Thus says the Lord: "Heaven is my throne, and the earth is my footstool; what is the house that you would build for me, and what is the place of my rest? All these things my hand has made, and so all these things came to be, declares the Lord. *But this is the one to whom I will look: he who is humble and contrite in spirit and trembles at my word.*"

If heaven is God's throne and the earth is his footstool, then that means God is big. Really, really BIG. So you're telling me, Isaiah, that my humility gets *his* attention? In the grand scheme of things my entire life is barely a blip on the radar screen. And my humility causes *God* to look my way? If that's the case, I wanted all the humility I could muster. But at that point I didn't even really know what humility was.

Once again, C. J. Mahaney came through, this time by defining humility in a way that helped me set my compass. "Humility is honestly assessing ourselves in light of God's holiness and our sinfulness." I read that definition again and again. I wrote it down and committed it to memory. Since then I don't think a day has gone by that I don't deliberately begin my day reminding myself of who God is in all his perfections and who I am as a sinner who commits sin. I make sure I get that straight and then I go the cross and rest there awhile. The blood in that place is bright red. It flows from the most glorious Person we can ever know. And grace is never far behind.

Phil and Euretta

8

Corridor to Glory

JOE

I have been face-to-face with federal agents twice in my life. Both times I was being interviewed because someone in our church was moving up in a government agency and needed a higher clearance. One time the agents reminded me of Will Smith and Tommy Lee Jones in the movie *Men in Black*. I kept waiting for them to bring out the little flashy thing and wipe out my short-term memory. Maybe they did. How would I know? The man who was receiving the higher clearance has since moved to Washington, D.C., where he undoubtedly has now become a Man in Black himself. His name is Bob or at least it was Bob the last time I saw him.

Bob came into a relationship with God while he was in the Navy serving on a submarine. He started reading the Bible from page one, which is something I don't normally recommend. I guess I have a lot more confidence in the New Testament actually holding someone's attention. There must be a dozen places in the Old Testament to get totally lost. But Bob began reading in Genesis. He said that by the time he got to Hosea he remembers thinking, *Wouldn't it be great if there really was a God like this?* When I first heard him say that I felt tears well up in my eyes. I am not sure why. Maybe it was because Hosea is a place where the love of God comes out with such force.

Hosea is a prophet who lives out the love of God by continuing to love his promiscuous wife Gomer. Hosea's pain is palpable in the story and yet he continues to pursue Gomer even going so far as to buy her back from prostitution. I can see a young man in a submarine curled up and reading these ancient words and suddenly feeling a longing in his soul for a God who would pursue him with such passion. Bob eventually made his way to the Gospels and knelt in the belly of a United States submarine and asked Jesus to be his Savior.

The Bible is a mysterious book. There are many times when I read the words printed on the tissue thin pages and they seem like any other words I read. Some sentences I understand, others are a little murky, but all in all it is a pretty uneventful experience. Then there are other times when the words take up a life of their own. They move through my eyes into my brain and then work their way through the invisible corridor to my soul where their little tails whip around driving each word deep into the fabric of who I really am. Once they worm their way in, there is no telling the damage or the healing they will eventually do.

My little brother John came to live with us one summer. He had just finished his sophomore year in college and my parents had moved to Birmingham, Alabama. John didn't know anyone in Birmingham so he got a job in Charlotte and lived with us. One weekend my wife decided to take the kids up to visit her grandmother in Ohio. John and I would be home alone and decided to make the most of a bachelor weekend. We cooked out, had some great conversation, and decided to have a Clint Eastwood movie marathon Monday night before Karen and the kids came back. John headed to work Monday morning and never came home. On the way home his motorcycle went left of center on a country road and plowed into a utility truck. He had been working with Tim, a fourteen-year-old from my youth group, and Tim was hitching a ride with John when they crashed. Two state troopers came to my house to tell me. John died at the scene. Tim was life-flighted to a local hospital and died en route.

When the troopers rang my doorbell I knew it was not going to be good. I walked out onto the front steps and after they told me I just sat down. They kept asking if I was going to be okay and to be honest I had no idea if I would be or not. The phone rang inside and it was Tim's mom who could feel in her bones that something was wrong. She was the first one I had to tell. No one really knows the power of words until you deliver that kind of news to a mother. After that call I made three more just like it. I called my wife, my dad, and then my older brother Brian. I heard the words break my dad's heart. Brian yelled like I had struck him. My wife began the journey home to be with me the moment she heard.

At the end of the Sermon on the Mount Jesus talked of two houses. One house was built upon sand and the other upon a rock. Jesus warned that a house built upon sand would not fare well in a storm. I had always thought my faith was built upon a rock, but in the midst of that storm my house split into pieces and the debris just floated out to sea.

In the Old Testament there are stories of families with household gods. The story of Rachel and Jacob is laced with deceit, and right at the end Rachel gets the best of Laban, her father, when she steals the household god and carries it away to another land. I realized as I stood knee deep in the aftermath of the storm, my faith floating like so many splinters around me, that I really had nothing more than a household god. As a minister and the son of a minister I thought I had a contract with God. My family would serve him and in exchange he would take care of us. It seemed like a no-brainer to me. I found out on that Monday night that God had not signed the contract and without a contract a household god is pretty worthless. I picked my god up and threw him as far as I could.

⌒

In Luke 15, Jesus begins a story by saying, "A father had two sons." One son lived in the father's house but ended up outside and one ran away from the father only to end up back in the house at the end of the story. The prodigal son is the younger son and takes up the majority of the story so most people focus on him. He tells the father that he wants his share of the inheritance. It was his way of telling the father that he wanted the father's stuff but not the father. The father obliges. The younger son then runs as far away from the father as he can and spends his inheritance on what the story calls riotous living.

When I first went to college I was like the younger son. I spent my freshman year running as far away from God as I could possibly run. Like many freshmen I spent that first year in a moral freefall. In Jesus' story the younger son finally comes to his senses in a pigpen and makes his way back to his father's house. His idea is that he will offer to work off his debt to the father as a hired hand. The father has different plans. When the father sees the son he runs to him and throws his arms around him. Before the son can finish his rehearsed apology the father reinstates him and shouts the plans for a huge party. The younger son is undone and for the first time in his life really sees his father and experiences the goodness and the love he had ignored for so long.

On a Saturday in September after a full year of riotous living I jumped in my car to head home for a weekend. I was weary of my life and myself. I told God I missed him and I wanted to come home. The Father ran to me that morning and threw his arms around me. It was the first time I ever really experienced God as Father and it changed me forever.

But in Jesus' story the father has two sons. The older son had been living in the father's house the whole time. He was out working in the field when he heard the sound of the homecoming party for his little brother. It infuriated him. When the father came out to try to encourage him to come to the house, the older brother went off. Basically he told the father that the younger son didn't deserve diddly while making it abundantly clear that he had been working all his life and the father owed him big time. What's fair is fair after all.

I had always seen myself as the younger brother. But by the time my own little brother was killed I had been working in the Father's fields for a while. I had forgotten the day he ran to me, hugged me and threw a party for my homecoming. Instead, in the midst of the storm I told God I deserved better. I told him he owed me, and I sat outside and sulked for nearly two years.

⌒‿⌐

At the end of those two years I was terribly lonely. I missed the Father. This was the first time I realized the power and the mystery of Holy Scripture. The words that years before had crossed the invisible corridor from mind to soul began to move and push deeper. God needed only two words to thaw my heart and bring me back home. The words came from the Gospel of John. "Jesus wept."[22] That was all it took.

I sat one night alone in my living room thinking about my brother with my throat tight and tears just behind my eyes and I remembered the first verse I had ever memorized as a boy. It is stuck right in the middle of the story of Jesus and Lazarus. Lazarus and Jesus had been friends. Actually Jesus was friends with the whole family which included not only Lazarus but also his two sisters, Mary and Martha. Lazarus got sick and his sisters sent word to Jesus. Jesus came late and by the time he showed up Lazarus was already in the grave and all hope was gone. Mary and Martha both thought Jesus had blown it and told him so. Jesus was about to pull a rabbit out of his hat and raise Lazarus back to life. Before he did though he walked over to the grave, knelt, and began to sob. That part never made much sense to me before. Why would Jesus cry? Why not be smiling like the cat who ate the canary when he knew he would have dinner with Lazarus and his sisters later that night? But Jesus wept between two worlds, the world he created and the world yet to be. In this in-between world brothers die and Jesus cried.

I sat in my living room and began to love him again. "There was a father who had two sons." The story is not just about the younger son, the prodigal. It is not just about the older son, the ingrate. And it is not just about two sons screwing up in different ways. It is about the father who would allow his heart to be broken by both sons. I began to love God again because the words that bore their way into my soul revealed the heart of the Father. I picked up a Bible and read these words in Psalm 62:11. "Two things do I know, two things have I heard. That you O Lord are loving and that you O God are strong." I have loved him ever since.

BOB

Phil and Euretta stopped me after church, introduced themselves, and asked about the little Bible study we held in our basement on Sunday nights. From the moment I laid eyes on them I sensed there was something peculiar about them. Halfway through our conversation I thought I had figured it out. There were smiles on their faces, and yet they weren't really smiling. It was like they were keeping a secret. Phil said he heard I had an extensive collection of Ohio State football memorabilia. I told him about my authentic 2002 National Championship helmet. It's autographed by Coach Jim Tressel. From that point on, we talked Buckeye.

We all know people who conceal their pain and sadness. They mask it over with empty smiles and small talk. I invited Phil and Euretta to visit our Bible study. But I also invited Phil to meet me for coffee. I felt a connection with him and a desire to go deeper. To maybe see what he was hiding. To see if he needed some help.

Phil showed up at Starbuck's the next morning wearing the same peculiar smile. I leaned back in my chair and asked him how he was doing.

"You don't know about Euretta, do you?"

"I guess not."

"Euretta's dying. She has terminal liver cancer. She's got about two or three months to live."

His words landed on me like bricks. I gulped and scrambled for something to say. But Phil wasn't done yet.

"To tell you the truth, we're both good with it. In fact we're really, really good."

For the next hour Phil talked and I hung on every word. It turned out the peculiar smile *was* concealing something. But it was the opposite of what I expected. It was joy, not sadness that was leaking through his face. Phil and Euretta were living between two worlds. And they had found something I'd been looking for all my life. I laughed at myself when I realized Phil didn't need my help. I needed his. So I did the logical thing and asked him to lead our Bible study the following Sunday.

I've heard Joe speak about his little brother's death many times. I can't even imagine what it must have been like on that doorstep with the State Troopers. Phil and Euretta's pain and loss were similar to Joe's only theirs was suspended in time. Almost in slow motion. And it was unfolding right before my eyes.

I have never personally experienced that kind of life-changing pain and loss. At least not yet. I know my time is coming. Almost no one gets through life unscathed. It's very rare to hear of anyone living a comfortable, secure life from beginning to end, and then dying in their sleep with a little smile on their face.

Many people go through tragic events and never recover. The pain and loss destroys them. But for others it's just the opposite. Intense suffering becomes part of a process that makes them stronger and more alive. I want to be like that. That's why I lean in close and listen hard to people like Joe and Phil and Euretta.

Sunday night came and the basement was packed. Phil and Euretta were the last to arrive. He had to help her down the steps. By the time she got to her seat, Euretta was exhausted. It had been one of those "bad days" where she was weak to the point of being limp. She cradled the right side of her belly with both arms. Euretta was in obvious pain as I opened with a prayer and introduced our guests. Phil started off by telling the group about Euretta's condition. He choked back tears as he described how close they were and how much he was going to miss her when she was gone. As his words sputtered out of his quivering lips, I noticed it again. Phil was smiling. I looked at Euretta. Underneath the tears welling up in her eyes was an unmistakable joy.

Phil took a cloth handkerchief out of his hip pocket, blew his nose like a foghorn and carefully cleaned out his nostrils. If he was trying to provide a moment of comic relief, it worked.

Then Phil opened up his Bible and got down to business. He talked about the glory of Christ for a solid hour. As the evening progressed, it was as if Christ emerged and Phil and Euretta disappeared. But the message between the lines was crystal clear. The two of them had begun to see Christ as the infinitely glorious Person whose presence overshadowed all their pain and loss. And the result was joy.

To our amazement, Phil asked Euretta to speak. She took a deep breath, stood up, and slowly made her way toward the front. Pain leaked through her smile. She could barely speak. We all leaned in. She told us that after she was diagnosed they went through weeks of the normal emotions and struggles. But then someone gave them John Piper's little article, "Don't Waste Your Cancer."[23] And that's when everything changed.

"As soon as we read it the lights went on. We realized that life is not our all-surpassing treasure. Christ is." Her eyes brightened as she spoke. "He's your treasure too, whether you realize it or not." You could hear a pin drop. She continued, "Phil and I cherish each other. We really do. We are soul mates. But we cherish Christ more. We have found him to be our goal and our reward. He is not a means to an end. He *is* the End." She was talking about a person, not an idea. "Cancer is hard, but not really. Living without Christ, now *that's* hard." Euretta was out of breath. But she wasn't done yet. "God's gifts are great, but we treasure the Giver above the gifts." That was her way of saying she wanted the Father, not just his stuff. Phil got up and stood by her side. He seemed to know she had one more point to make. But instead of taking over, he asked us to give her a moment. The room went silent for several minutes as we marveled and waited, wondering what deep secret of life would light up the basement next.

Euretta picked up her Bible and opened it. Her voice was weak but her words were strong, "Two verses explain this better than I can." She did not need to look at her Bible. She spoke slowly because she didn't want us to miss a single word. "I count everything as loss because of the surpassing worth of knowing Christ Jesus my Lord . . . To live is Christ, and to die . . . is GAIN."[24] Euretta's eyes were ablaze as she repeated the sacred words a second time. And then she sat down.

Joe talked about arriving at a place where he experienced the power and the mystery of Holy Scripture. Euretta was living in that place.

⌒

A couple weeks later Phil started an on-line journal to keep everyone informed. I copied some excerpts and I'll share them in chronological order. Lean in close and listen hard and I bet you'll find something here that sticks to your soul.

These days are special because Euretta and I seem to exist inside God's cocoon of hard-to-fathom love.

⌒

Euretta looks so good and healthy. Actually, she looks more beautiful than ever. From the outside she appears to be in the second trimester of pregnancy—a happy-looking mom-to-be. Inside, growing tumors smash against her other organs in a battle to completely shut down her liver. Ah, but there's something else glowing inside Euretta. It is her neon-white soul, made pure and spotless by the redemptive power of her Savior's horrific crucifixion and glorious resurrection.

~

Last night as I was trying to pray before falling asleep, I heard Euretta's emotion-filled voice proclaim, "Philip, these past two years have been the happiest years of my life."

~

Wednesday, March 25, doesn't exist for Euretta. It never happened. She jumped over Wednesday like a chess knight jumping over a pawn. That's because Euretta spent the day hallucinating. Looking back, Wednesday turned out to be quite funny and I wanted to preserve the wacky comments Euretta unknowingly made:

"Santa Claus is re-arranging our bathroom furniture."

"Philip, I don't think we should live in a wet sock drawer."

During the evening news she said she was watching the shopping channel. I told her she was watching Betsy Kling giving the weather report and she replied, "Yes, but she is selling boobies." It was a day of comic relief as we crawl toward the finish line. The absolute wonderful thing is that we know the victorious outcome because each and every promise from God is true.

~

What has yet to happen is the denouement of Euretta's life-book. But we already firmly and absolutely joyously know what it is. It was determined two thousand years ago. On a cross.

~

In bed this morning Euretta mumbled strange phrases like, "I have butter sticks in my bed." She suddenly paused as a heart-felt, tender, endearing expression painted her face. Then she prophesied, "One of these days soon you will walk into this room and I won't be here." At this my brain turned to oil. This lasted for hours—a new low in my melancholy department. Lest you think this is a day of self-pity let me tell you of the other side of the coin. The joy-compensating side. John Piper wrote, "When God calls us to suffer he is not calling us away from joy but into joy."

Phil ended each of his journal entries the same way. "Savoring Christ, Phil." That in itself spoke volumes.

Our little group grew very close to Phil and Euretta as the end drew near. Between the pain and the pain medication, Euretta wasn't able to talk much. She didn't need to. Her eyes told the story. Phil continued to focus on the glory of Christ. One day the telephone rang and it was Phil. "She's with him now." I asked him how he was. "I'm good with it. Really, really good." A familiar smile was in his voice.

Phil and I got together at Starbuck's the day before Euretta's funeral. Somehow the stoning of Stephen came up, so we went to Acts 7. Stephen did not have terminal liver cancer, but he did face a certain death. Picture this. An enraged mob "ground their teeth at him." Phil asked what that meant. "I'm not sure," I said, "but it sounds like their heads were about to explode." Next, they "picked up stones to stone him." I knew what that meant—they were going to bash Stephen's head in with rocks. I read the next section out loud and discovered that a spirit-filled Stephen "gazed into heaven and saw the glory of God, and Jesus standing at the right hand of God. And he said, 'Behold, I see the heavens opened, and the Son of Man standing at the right hand of God.'"[25]

Phil said, "Wait a minute. I thought Jesus was *seated* at the right hand of God."

"He is," I replied, remembering Hebrews 1:3.

"But this says Jesus was *standing*. It even says it twice. That can only mean one thing." Phil's entire face broke into an enormous smile. "At the very moment my Euretta died, she saw the heavens opened. And the Son of God got up from his throne to greet her."

Phil jumped to his feet. "Can you imagine? Jesus sat watching this whole process and then stood up just for her! To welcome her home!"

Joe wrote that there are times when the words of the Bible take up a life of their own. For Phil and me, this was one of those times.

"Do you think Stephen felt the rocks?" Phil asked, with Euretta in mind.

Phil sat down and thought for a moment. But then the smile returned and he sprang back to his feet. He pointed his finger, putting it almost on my nose and replied, "Yeah, he felt them, but I bet you couldn't tell by the look on his face."

Stephen did not waste his stoning. And Euretta did not waste her cancer. Their overwhelming desire for God transformed their terminal afflictions into deeply satisfying, God-glorifying, personal experiences and public testimonies. It transformed their loss into gain. That's the way I want to go, too.

⁓

Euretta's funeral was on a Saturday. No one expected Phil to come to Bible study the next night. But he did. He was the first to show up and the last to leave. He said our little group had become his family. In the weeks that followed, Phil continued to be an inspiration to us all. And every week he admired more of my Buckeye paraphernalia. You see, he and Euretta were alums, charter members of the Buckeye Nation.

Six weeks after Euretta died, I asked Phil to lead the study for us. We were going through the Gospel of John and were up to verse 6 of chapter 1. He agreed to cover the next three verses. But on Friday afternoon he called with a question.

"I'm not getting much out of the section you assigned, so would it be okay if I covered verse fourteen instead?" I agreed.

"Good," he said, "I'll get right on it since the study is the day after tomorrow."

My cell phone rang the next morning. It was our founding pastor, Jim Colledge. He told me Phil was dead.

"You know, Bob, I went into the bedroom and I noticed something amazing—Phil died in his sleep with a little smile on his face."

I told Jim I knew why. I knew what Phil was thinking about when he climbed into bed for the last time. The mysterious power of John 1:14 had been moving through Phil's eyes into his brain. It worked its way through the invisible corridor of his soul. "And the Word became flesh and dwelt among us, and we have seen his glory, glory as of the only Son from the Father, full of grace and truth." In the moments prior to his death, like Stephen and Euretta, Phil saw the glory of Christ. And he smiled so hard some of it stuck on his face even after he was dead.

Our little Bible study group met the next night. The right side of the couch where Phil always sat was empty. And we decided to dub John 1:14 "Phil's Verse."

Karen and Joe

9

The Math of God

JOE

I don't think I have a problem recognizing there are people who are much smarter than I am. I picked up a book on Socratic logic because I thought it would be a good place to start with philosophy. I realized fairly quickly I am the type of person who needs someone to explain philosophy to me and hopefully draw pictures as they do. I think realizing some people are smarter than you is an important part of becoming a likeable human being. There are a couple of people I know who haven't gotten to that place and frankly I don't think anyone likes them very much.

My problem is more with God. It is not that I don't think God is smarter than I am, it is just that I don't often think of God as being brilliant. I have read plenty of books on systematic theology. The sections on the nature of God are my favorite but they always leave a category out. They don't really leave it out; they just name it omniscience which doesn't really do much for me. Omniscience means that God is all-knowing, whatever that means. In the movie *Good Will Hunting*, Matt Damon plays a genius who is a tough kid from south Boston. In one scene he dresses down a Harvard yuppie in a local bar. After the yuppie walks away humiliated, Matt Damon's friend looks at a girl who has witnessed the intellectual beating and says in his thick Boston accent, "My friend is wicked smart." Sometimes I don't need someone to tell me God is omniscient, I need someone to remind me he is wicked smart.

I sit with people fairly often who are trying to figure God out. It's funny—no one needs to figure God out on their wedding day or when they get a promotion. When things are going well we can all agree God is doing a splendid job running the universe. But when pain hits hard enough nearly everyone I know begins to ask questions about God. They are the same questions I asked when my little brother died on the side of a country road. I would guess the questions have not changed much through the centuries.

The questions that arise from a soul on fire are simple ones. Pain tends to distill thinking into simple equations. Pleasure is good and pain is bad. Life is good and death is bad. Health is good and sickness is bad. I was going to say the list could go on but it really doesn't have to. That pretty much covers it. It is what I call the simple math of life. If you want to know if you are a simple mathematician when it comes to life you just need to listen to the prayers you pray to God. We ask God to give safe travels, to bless the food, to give us a good day, to heal the people we know and care about. When God decides to do something else I wonder if he heard my earnest prayers, or worse yet, forgot the simple math of life. Did God forget that pleasure is good and pain bad and that is why I had such a horrendous day or year or decade? How hard are those equations to remember? Is God a moron or maybe standing impotently behind the curtain like the Wizard of Oz?

⌒

A little girl was born without a right hand. Her parents went through all the questions. Who wouldn't? How hard is the equation there? She went through grade school with a prosthetic hook. You can imagine the pain she endured from classmates when *Peter Pan* became the hit movie of the year. I met her when I was a sophomore in college. She was stunning and there was a depth in her I did not see in other girls. I married her. Karen has a rare combination of compassion and strength that only comes from suffering. She is like steel wrapped in velvet. I have told her many times that I didn't marry her in spite of her arm, I married her because of her arm. I am not sure she believes me. It is always easier to see how character is formed in others than it is in yourself. Karen still believes she would be the same person inside if she had been born with two hands and hadn't gone through the fire that only she knows. She is wrong. She would not be the same.

The Math of God is much more complex than our simple math. In our math things like health and life and pleasure are the end of the equation. They are the sum, the goal. For God those things are simply variables. Health is a variable but then so is sickness. Pleasure is a variable but so is pain.

I first met my friend Dave in the dead of winter. He was wearing shorts. If you live in the south or out west it may not seem like a big deal but here in northeastern Ohio it is not something you see every day. Dave played football for Purdue and has maintained some of the girth necessary to be a lineman in college football. Dave is one of the most interesting and complex guys I know. He has started several companies including one during the "dot com" boom that should have netted him several hundred million. He and the capital investor thought the offer of $700 million was a little low. By the time they got another offer the tech bubble had burst and so had their fledgling company. He told me this with very little regret. Dave has a lot of life in him and not much regret. It seems he is running through life looking straight ahead and not looking back. I like Dave and have since the first time I met him. He carries himself with the same combination of strength and tenderness I see in my wife every day. It seems incongruous for an ex-football player of his size. Every fiber of his being seems intent on doing something of value. If he does ever make a hundred million the world will be much better for it.

Not too long ago Dave told me about his dad. When Dave was in his twenties, his dad had a massive stroke. He lived but did not speak for the next eighteen years. Dave spent a lot of time caring for his mom and dad over those years. He put his dad on the board of his company just to have him close. I have no idea what that kind of pain did inside Dave's dad or his mom. But I can see what it did inside Dave. He would never have chosen that path for himself and yet he could not be anything close to the man he is now without traveling that terribly steep path.

I am not so naïve to think that pain always has a positive impact on character. Pain is a storm and I have seen people twisted, broken, and made bitter by the sheer force. When I sit in my office with someone who questions God, they are always questioning one of two parts of God. They question his heart or his head. "Either God does not love me enough to do good things in my life or God doesn't really know what I need and it seems pretty damn simple from where I am standing."

I love reading J. R. R. Tolkien. If you have read the *Lord of the Rings* trilogy, you know Tolkien writes at multiple levels. You may or may not know that embedded in the story is a composite Christ. Each of the heroes of the story takes on a slice of Jesus and if you put them all together like a jigsaw puzzle you can see him. Aragorn is the king come disguised as Strider only to be revealed in glory at the end. Frodo carries the burden of the world to Mount Doom. Sam walks with Frodo every step of the way. Gandalf sacrifices his life only to resurrect and return. So, not only does Tolkien create an entire elf language, construct the prehistory of Middle Earth, and weave one of the most magnificent stories every penned, he also adds in the gospel for those who have eyes to see.

Tolkien was wildly smart. I just can't see myself going up to J. R. R. Tolkien and questioning his ability to think through a situation. In the same way I can't see myself going up to Mother Teresa and questioning her love for the poor and downtrodden. Can you see yourself walking into a hospice in the slums of Calcutta in your pressed western clothes and demanding that Mother Teresa explain herself because you really don't think she cares enough?

At the end of the book of Job, God seems to tear into Job. Job has been questioning both God's heart and his head and finally it seems God has had enough. Job is demanding an answer to the Why question. He wants God to explain his math. Instead, God launches into a series of questions for Job. The scene is both wonderful and terrible at the same time. It is wonderful in that the God of the universe will address the little ancient man sitting on an ash heap after losing just about everything. It is terrible in that the power and glory God unleashes in a series of questions is unequaled in all of Scripture. He asks Job dozens of questions Job cannot begin to answer. The barrage seems endless. Finally, when God brings the interrogation to a close, Job sputters out an apology. In some ways God seems like a cosmic bully. Why does he do it? The reason is that deep down Job didn't need God's math explained. He wouldn't understand it anyway. Neither would you. Job needed God himself. He needed to be reminded that God is brilliant. That God is writing at multiple levels in multiple lives at every moment. I find myself needing to be reminded of God's brilliance too. But I also need to be reminded of his heart.

I remember hearing Brennan Manning speak one time. He painted a picture of coming up behind Mary as she watched her son hang on the cross. In Manning's story we come up behind her and ask her a simple question, "Mary, do you think your son really loves me?" Mary turns and looks at us with tears staining her face and says simply, "What more could he have done for you?" Indeed.

Pain tempts me to question the heart or the head of God. I only need to take a look in either a telescope or a microscope to be reminded of his head. I only need to take a look at the cross to be reminded of his heart. God, forgive me for my simple math.

BOB

I almost majored in mathematics at Ohio State. I've always enjoyed math, especially calculus. The essence of calculus is trying to discover and apply the unfathomable meaning of infinity. Whenever I concentrated hard on calculus something cool always happened—I'd get a strange and wonderful feeling of self-forgetfulness. Because a glimpse of bigness always made me feel small in a good way.

So when Joe came up with the idea for this chapter, I figured it would be right up my alley. But as I struggled to think of a way to contribute, I started to feel like Russell Crowe going crazy in *A Beautiful Mind*. That's because the Math of God makes calculus look like kindergarten arithmetic. Understanding the Math of God is humanly impossible. "For my thoughts are not your thoughts, neither are your ways my ways," declares the Lord. "For as the heavens are higher than the earth, so are my ways higher than your ways and my thoughts than your thoughts."[26] David wrote, "Such knowledge is too wonderful for me; it is high, I cannot attain it."[27]

And yet I find myself hungry to grasp something of God's math. To move beyond simple, me-centered math. I'm drawn in by an almost innate awareness that God's math is beautiful, majestic, and perfect. That it continually surrounds and envelops every one of us. That even though it is ultimately beyond our reach, there are knowable parts of some of the equations—for those who have eyes to see.

Sorry to say, I don't have much insight to offer. I'll share the little bit I have figured out so far. Here are three corollaries I've managed to collect:

1. God's math is always profound and paradoxical. Whenever you realize things are not what they seem to be, you're probably learning God's math. Here are some mind-boggling examples of single-sentence paradoxical equations straight from the Bible:

   It is more blessed to give than to receive.[28]

   The greatest among you shall be your servant.[29]

   For whoever would save his life will lose it.[30]

   You meant evil against me, but God meant it for good.[31]

   When I am weak, then I am strong.[32]

   The Bible is a veritable God-math textbook. You'll find it's full of stuff like this. I'll give you a sub-corollary: take your time with it because if you're in too much of a hurry, the Math of God will blow right past you.
2. Brokenness is a constant in God's formulas. Our brokenness forms the cracks through which grace flows in and joy pours out. Learning the Math of God involves embracing brokenness the way he does. It involves a collision between his grace and our brokenness.
3. The resultant sum of all of God's calculations is the same: We get more of him. Getting more of God equals finding satisfaction, significance, and fulfillment in him. When we do, it is axiomatic: we get more joy and God gets more glory. And that results in living a life that transcends circumstances.

I know it's not much, but it's a start. Fortunately, I have crossed paths with several people who have dabbled in advanced God-math. One is my mentor, Jerry Bridges. But I'm saving him for a later chapter. For now, I'll share my experiences with two other God-math whizzes.

In 2005, Amy and I attended a weekend conference called *Suffering and the Sovereignty of God*. One of the speakers had been a quadriplegic for forty years after suffering a spinal cord injury from a diving accident when she was sixteen. Joni Eareckson Tada endured unimaginable hardship and I wanted to see her, not just hear her. So I made the effort to get us good seats. By my standards I was only moderately successful—we made it to the front row, but we were too far off to the side.

I cheered up when the musicians arrived on stage to lead worship. I realized we had a perfect angle to see Joni waiting backstage in her turbo-powered wheelchair. Halfway through the first song, I noticed the wheelchair begin to wobble. Moments later it started spinning around. I got nervous. Then it dawned on me. Joni, the quadriplegic, was wheelchair dancing! Watching Joni backstage spoke volumes. She gave new meaning to the word *joystick*.

That night Joni provided a lesson in the Math of God at the quantum mechanics level. She was like a professor writing equations in words on the chalkboards of our minds. One of her sentences seemed to come at me in slow motion. "When suffering lobs a hand grenade your way, your soul may be blasted bare, you may feel raw and come undone—but you then can be better bonded to the Savior." As she spoke, it felt like I was getting blown out of a foxhole. Like I was suspended upside-down in midair.

When I snapped out of it, Joni was talking about her experience of joy in the midst of suffering. "And then God happily shares his gladness, his joy flooding over heaven's walls, filling your heart in a waterfall of delight which then streams out to others in a flood of encouragement and then erupts back to God in an ecstatic fountain of praise. He imparts a new way of looking at your hardships. He puts a song in your heart."

At this point I glanced at Amy as if to say, "Is this lady for real?" Amy raised her eyebrows as if to say, "She is." But it turned out Joni was just getting warmed up. The next thing we knew, she literally broke out into song. You can watch the entire fifty-minute message for free.[33] If you watch it, note the way she ends the session with a resounding description of hope. She gets the crowd to join her in singing the old hymn, "Solid Rock," that begins, "My hope is built on nothing less than Jesus' blood and righteousness." As the audience stands to lift up the words, the lights are slowly dimmed. By the middle of the song the only light in the room came from the words on the screens. At the end of the song, the lights went back up and no one knew what to do because Joni was nowhere to be found. In the darkness she had silently motored off the stage, making sure there'd be no applause, no standing ovation for Joni. She had applied a God-math principle right before our eyes.

Life is made up of a series of little events with an occasional big event thrown in. Breaking your neck like Joni did is a huge event, but it doesn't happen every day. Certainly God's math works on this level, the macro level—he numbers the stars and calls them all by name. But it also works on the micro level—the very hairs of your head are all numbered. God's math is at work beneath the surface of seemingly insignificant events. In the mundane, ordinary events of everyday life.

The first person I ever heard describe God as *brilliant* was Rob Thomas. I've also heard him call God elegant, majestic, regal, insurmountable, and enthralling. Rob has an aura of glee. He's like a kid in a candy store, which is a weird analogy because Rob is sixty years old and a lanky six foot three. And he can beat me in tennis.

Rob is one of the most extraordinary people I have ever met. Yet from all outward appearances he's an ordinary man, living an ordinary life, in an ordinary house, with an ordinary family. He has an ordinary job. Rob is an elementary school custodian. A janitor. Rob is extraordinary because he understands the Math of God on a micro level. His day-to-day life consists of a series of remarkable, almost non-stop experiences of relationship with God in the midst of utterly unremarkable circumstances.

111

Rob is a charter member of our little Sunday night Bible study group. He attends week after week, quietly listening as others lead the discussion. Rob prefers not to lead. But fortunately for us, something inevitably happens to get him going, and Rob starts gushing God's math. Sometimes he gets downright giddy over it. We all lean in, hoping some of it will rub off on us. But most of what he says goes right over our heads.

Rob cleans houses on the side. Ours is one of them. Since we no longer have a big home we don't really need a cleaning service, but we do it as an excuse to have Rob around. Rob is like a pastor making a house call who happens to clean your toilets in the process. One day I noticed he was in the zone with the vacuum cleaner. Suddenly he started laughing to himself. He was almost belly-laughing. I yanked the plug out of the socket and asked what was up. "Oh," he said, with a hint of embarrassment, "It was nothing. I was just chuckling to the Lord about the peace I have in cleaning houses. How much to do, how much not to do. I remembered how when I first started I was anxious about stuff like whether I was working fast enough, doing a good enough job, whether I could make enough money. I was sharing a giggle with the Lord about it and an old blues song covered by Stevie Ray Vaughn came to mind, 'The Things [That] I Used to Do.' Well I don't do 'em any more. The Lord has provided me with a virtual PhD in the nuts and bolts of cleaning. I got so overcome with gratitude for that, it felt like I was dancing—but I was just vacuuming the floor!"

Recently, I sat down with Rob to try to capture some corollaries on the micro-level of God's math. I pointed out the insignificance of the little daily tasks we all undertake in life. Rob's eyes got big as he exclaimed, "It doesn't matter whether it's big or small in the world's eyes, if God is moving in my life in any way at all—it's HUGE!"

I asked him how he avoids getting bored at work. He quickly replied. "I'm beside myself with the goodness of the Lord. It's like the old Beatle's song. It's 'Here, There and Everywhere.' " That was his answer. I waited for more. But that was it.

I asked Rob what goes through his mind as he's driving to the school. I hit a gusher with that one. "I'm in the habit of rehearsing the gospel and reveling in his love. I meditate on it. I'm consumed with his outrageous mercy. I'm obsessed with his unfathomable grace. I'm fascinated, enchanted, and dumbstruck by the good news of the cross. I feel drenched in his precious blood and clothed in his perfect righteousness. I sense the presence and glory of Christ. When I get to the school, my cup runneth over and I love the teachers, the children, and the parents. Mother Theresa said, 'If you see someone without a smile, give them yours.' So that's what I do. And almost without thinking I become an instrument that transmits his love even though no words are spoken."

I asked about the role Scripture plays in developing his math skills. His face grew intense. "I can't pick up the Bible and read it without feeling like the guys on the road to Emmaus—my heart burns within me. I come unglued. I start wigging out with joy." Rob loves to describe Bible verses as *delicious*. I thought that was weird until he pointed out Jeremiah 15:16 which he quotes from the King James Version, "Thy words were found, and I did eat them; and thy word was unto me the joy and rejoicing of mine heart."

Mark Phipps is a highly analytical structural engineer. He started coming to our Sunday night Bible study. After a couple weeks he asked me if Rob was for real. "Check him out," I said. So Mark started meeting with Rob, watching him closely, looking for cracks. Not surprisingly, he found some. Rob is not perfect. But Mark made a surprising observation—there was obvious joy coming out of Rob's brokenness. Mark asked him to explain, and he recorded what Rob told him. Here it is, word-for-word: "Oh, I've got plenty of cracks all right. In fact I'm constantly broken over my own wretched, miserable sin. That's why the joy you are asking about is my greatest joy of all—glorying in the cross."

I showed Rob what Joe wrote about the Math of God. He grinned, "It's funny. I knew Karen Coffey for years before I noticed she had a prosthetic hand." I asked Rob to add to Joe's description of simple math to bring it down to the ordinary events of life. His answer went like this: "Simple math says money and comfort and security and power and attractiveness are the goals, the end of the equations. But in God's math all these things are just variables. And so are living paycheck-to-paycheck, flat tires, kids with the flu, difficult bosses, birthmarks, indigestion, and zits. God uses 'em all. And when it comes to intelligence, simple math says bright is good, dull is bad. But the man with Down Syndrome who packs my groceries at the supermarket might have more joy and love for Jesus than anyone I know."

I asked Rob if he ever heard of Joni. He smiled and told me he'd been praying for her for years. "In fact," he added, "one day I got into a little squabble with the Lord over her. I was listening to Joni on the radio. She had bronchitis and could hardly breathe. She was practically gasping for air. I got a little upset with him. 'Lord, hasn't she been through enough?' The Lord replied, 'You have no idea what I am preparing for her.' Rob responded, 'O Lord, shut my mouth.' "

I told Rob a verse Joni quoted in her message. "For I consider that the sufferings of this present time are not worth comparing with the glory that is to be revealed to us."[34] Rob's eyes grew big and he said, "Yeah, and get a load of this one: 'Eye hath not seen, nor ear heard, neither have entered into the heart of man, the things which God hath prepared for them that love him'.[35] Factor that into the equation and it will take us a long, long way, won't it?"

There are no timelines in God's math. All things are now to him. I hope I remember that next time I question God's head or his heart. Both Joni and Rob speak a lot about heaven. I've concluded that the best God-mathematicians on earth are the heaven-minded ones.

As Rob left our home after the "interview," he turned around with a twinkle in his eye. "Remember the gospel—and don't forget to bask." He drove off and I got a feeling he had just given me the answer to the next pop quiz.

10

Eating Work and the Search for Satisfaction

JOE

Big Dan was the first man I ever met who ate work. We were sitting in his car. It was a brand new Lincoln Continental. Big Dan was old school, which means he liked American cars. He knew Germans made better engines but he said they had no idea how to make an interior. He was a Cadillac or Lincoln guy.

Dan's voice was a little hoarse, like someone on *The Sopranos*. I was the youth pastor at the church Dan and his family attended, and his son was struggling. In my opinion the son needed more of his dad and I was telling Dan this as we sat outside the church in the soft leather seats of his jet black Continental. Big Dan was a business owner. He looked at me and with his Soprano-like voice said, "I want you to know something, Joe. I do this all for him." I was too young and Big Dan was a little too scary for me to look him in the eye and tell him he was full of it. I wish I had. Maybe then his son would not have been nearly as lost as he became over the next few years.

Big Dan probably really believed he was working all those long hours for his son. But as we sat there in a brand new Lincoln

Continental there seemed to be some pretty good perks for dads who sacrifice for their families.

I have a theory that everyone eats something other than food to stay alive. We all have emotional needs as well as physical needs. Everyone knows what they eat physically because you can see it and then taste it going down. Emotional food is different but no less necessary. You will die without it. There seem to be two types of emotional food human beings need. Everyone needs to feel loved and everyone needs to feel important. Let's call it security and significance. My wife is a counselor. If a client says, "No one really cares about me" or "I really don't matter" then that rings an alarm. A human being who is not experiencing security or significance is starving emotionally and is in danger.

Every day we wake up hungry. We are hungry physically and we are hungry emotionally. Every day we must eat if we are going to survive.

Now, suppose that every time we ate something to fill our emotional tanks we could see it. Let's make the analogy easy. Say if every time we needed to feel loved we had to have a red M&M and every time we needed to feel important or significant we needed a green M&M. Love: red. Important: green. You would wake up in the morning and have a bowl of cereal and grab a handful of red and green M&Ms and you would be good to go. You would last until lunch at which time you would grab a sandwich and pull out a few red ones and green ones, smile, and finish up your day. When you got home you would eat dinner, pour yourself a glass of wine and munch on a few more red ones, feel all warm inside, and go to bed.

Red and green M&Ms would be the most important commodity in the entire world. Wars would be fought for red and green M&Ms. People would be mugged for trying to walk home with a little bag of red M&Ms. People would work long and hard hours and sacrifice their kids to be paid off with a baggie of green M&Ms every night. And there you have it.

Big Dan told me he was doing it all for his son. He said it with a straight face while green M&Ms spilled out of the glove compartment.

⌒‿‿

In my town most men quit working for money a while ago and started working for green M&Ms. There are a lot of big houses and nice cars where I live. If success really did provide security and significance my town would be filled with well-adjusted and happy people. I guess it's not working too well, because the counselors in our town are still really busy.

When men who don't know each other get together they usually have two introductory questions. "What is your name?" And "What do you do?" That's it. That's all we have before we start talking about sports. The second question is asked simply to find out who has more green M&Ms. If you have a higher paying or more respectable job than the man you are talking to then he has to give you a couple of green ones and that is just awesome. If you talk to someone who has a better job than you, then you have to give up some green ones and that really stinks. I know. I am a pastor. When I tell someone what I do the most common response is, "So, a pastor. Wow. That's great. Good for you." It's the same compliment you get for going with your daughter on the Little Princess camping weekend. The only thing missing is the head noogie. I have gotten used to it over time.

Ever since our church has grown I find myself enjoying pastor conferences immensely. Pastors love green M&Ms as much or more than everybody else. We are usually frozen out of the M&M free-for-all at the country club or neighborhood cocktail party so we make up for it when we get together with other pastors. It is hard to compare spirituality without really looking like an idiot so we go with straight up numbers. How big is your church? How many staff members do you have? Sometimes we are able to mask the question by asking about the number of services or campuses. Something seems really wrong with all this. The reason is that green M&Ms don't magically appear. Someone has to provide them. If I get some green M&Ms some poor guy just lost some. It is a zero-sum game. You would expect this to happen at corporate functions but when pastors play this game it's messed up.

I think Christians got turned sideways a while ago. Christians are now more widely known for what we don't do. That is a lousy way to be known. It has created an image of Christianity as a set of rules. I don't think that is what Jesus had in mind when he came and said, "If the Son sets free, you will be free indeed."[36] I think Jesus intended his followers to be wildly different, particularly in how they relate to security and significance. At the moment we are really good at spotting immorality and condemning it. But as far as distributing red and green M&Ms, we are about as stingy as everyone else, maybe worse.

I remember being at an orphanage in the Dominican Republic. The director pointed to a little boy being fed by a worker. He told me the little boy had just been rescued. He came from a family of eight. His parents didn't have enough money to feed everyone. At four years old he was the youngest and the last to eat. He slept on a little piece of foam rubber in the corner of the tiny shanty house. He was so hungry when he went to bed he would nibble on the foam to take away some of the pain. When he arrived at the orphanage he was starving but his belly was full.

I have a longing to feel valuable. Work seems to do that at least for a moment. But it never fills me up. Work does not seem to have the nutrients necessary to fill my emotional need for significance.

Adam worked the garden of Eden. Before he sinned and something broke inside him, I think he probably really enjoyed the garden. I don't think he used it to try to make himself more attractive to Eve. I don't think he neglected his marriage so he could work longer hours, clear more land, have a bigger and better garden to capture more market share. I see him in my mind's eye working the garden until he heard the rustling in the trees and realized the Lord had come by to check on him. I think he dropped the hoe and looked into the face of God, and it is that face that filled him to overflowing. We were not made to gain value from our work; we were made for the Face.

When Jesus was being crucified he cried out at one point. He had endured tremendous physical pain without uttering a sound but finally it was as if the dam burst and he screamed in agony. He arched his back and yelled, "My God, my God, why have you forsaken me." Jesus always had absolute intimacy with the Father. He had the Father's full attention, complete love, and absolute delight. Jesus always had the very Face of God. But at the moment when our sins were transferred onto Jesus, God the Father turned away from his Son and his Son screamed in absolute emptiness. Most people know that Jesus paid for our sins on the cross. That is true. But there's more to the story. He lost the Face temporarily here on earth so that we could have it forever in heaven.

Adam looked up at God and saw a face that was beaming. Adam knew he was the apple of God's eye and it filled him from head to toe with green M&Ms. And because of the cross, I, too, have become the apple of God's eye.

~

The need for significance is only surpassed by our desperate need for love. People who do not feel loved will do almost anything for a taste. The search for love can lead us to fill ourselves with that which does not satisfy. Teenage girls who are hungry for love are terribly vulnerable. Their desperation may push them toward really unhealthy relationships. Mothers may fill the void of love by serving their children. They rely on their children to feel loved but end up being slaves to children who have no intention of paying them back.

In the Gospel of John there is a story of a woman who runs into Jesus at a well outside of Sychar. During the course of the encounter we find that she has had five husbands and is now living with a man. Her whole life had been a search for a source of red M&Ms. With each new husband she had hoped to be filled with such love that she would finally be satisfied. Jesus looked at her and said, "If you knew the gift of God, and who it is that is saying to you, 'Give me a drink,' you would have asked him, and he would have given you living water."[37]

The love of Jesus is so amazing, so overwhelming, that you simply cannot come into contact with it and not be radically changed. You cannot be a real Christian without that love gripping you any more than you can jump into a swimming pool and not get wet.

Jesus claimed he came to provide us with life and that life was going to be abundant.[38] This life would flow out of us in a river of red and green. And then he went and died on a cross to give us that life.

We try to fill ourselves up with everything else. Big Dan, spending all those hours eating work, was still as hungry as the day he was born.

Jesus sat in an upper room the night before he died. He took some bread and tore it in two. He gave it to his disciples and said, "Take, eat. This is my body which is given for you."[39] Take and eat he said. If you are ever really going to be filled, it will be with this. Out of all the ways Jesus could have given us to remember him he chose to give us something to eat. Eat, and remember the cross. Eat, and remember the love. Eat, and remember the Face of the One who fills all in all.

BOB

I used to eat work. At the height of my entrepreneurial era I worked sixteen-hour days, seven days a week. I was driven by visions of storehouses of green M&Ms. After two years of that I cashed out and bought my dream home. But Joe already covered the work-related aspect of M&Ms with his story about Big Dan. So I'd like to explore a more intriguing aspect. Sex.

When I was a sophomore in high school I dated a junior named Monique. That is not her real name but I chose it as a pseudonym because it seemed like a good fit. "Monique" was indisputably the most physically attractive girl at Cuyahoga Falls High School. She'd walk down the hall and all the guys' heads would turn and then they would start crying. The girls called her a bimbo, but she was actually very intelligent. She got the bimbo label because she did a little modeling to make money for college. She got hired to go to car shows and sit on the hoods of muscle cars dressed in a white string bikini. Quite the hood ornament, that Monique.

Our relationship started in Advanced Creative Writing class. By some incredible stroke of luck the teacher paired us up on a project. We visited a nearby cemetery and wrote poetry in the spring sunshine. There was a magical moment that day among the tombs when she fell deeply "in love" with me while I fell even more deeply in lust with her.

I didn't have a car back then so I'd walk Monique home after school. I carried her books and held her hand while shiny new dump trucks pulled up and buried me in green M&Ms. My friends from the football team were the truck drivers. They couldn't believe this was happening to me. Neither could I. While I enjoyed a steady stream of massive quantities of green M&Ms, I occasionally offered Monique a few fake red ones. In spite of her beauty I did not truly love her.

I was a virgin but she was not. One afternoon we were in my basement making out on the couch and she whispered, "I wish you would touch me." Since I was already touching her when she said that, I figured she must have had something else in mind. At age seventeen she had already developed a significant appetite for sex. And thanks to Joe I now know why. She was starving for red M&Ms. I consider it a minor miracle that my virginity made it through that day still intact.

Fast-forward thirty-five years. I ran into Monique's brother. His update on her made me sad. Turns out the relational pattern

I experienced with her repeated itself for decades. She never found love. Relationships never lasted. Her life was eventually commandeered by an addiction. Right now she's somewhere in California—alone. It could all be explained by a lack of red M&Ms and the fact that she never quite found the Face of the Father.

⌒

Addictions start when you don't get enough M&Ms, so you detach your desire for them and re-attach it to something else. That "something else" becomes the object of your addiction and you begin to fill up on it. It may be alcohol or drugs, but it could also be golf, or TV, or a person, or food, or having an attractive body, or peer group approval, or _____. We all have something. It's the thing you turn to for security and significance. The thing you need in order to have a good day. The thing you can't live without.

As addictions develop, your appetite for M&Ms begins to fade. And that begins to wreak havoc on your relationships. You begin to lose the emotional connections that result from the normal sharing of M&Ms. Eventually you don't even care. The process goes on and you end up like Monique, alone in your own little world.

Addictions also wreak havoc on your relationship with God. The object of your addiction replaces the Face of the Father. It becomes your idol—you bow down and worship it. It becomes your master—you listen and obey. Meanwhile the real God, the One who created you, gets lip service at best. That's why addictive behaviors are acts of cosmic treason. Sin on steroids.

Not surprisingly, the object of your addiction gradually takes over your identity. Anonymous organizations for addicts know this well. In AA you say, "My name is _____ and I am an alcoholic." But this applies to any object of addiction. "I am a _____" —a smoker; an anorexic; a millionaire; a homosexual; a blackjack player; a chocoholic; a hard body; a sports fan-atic. You become one with it. If you're proud of it you have stuff like T-shirts or bumper stickers to herald who you are. If you're ashamed of it you keep it in the closet, a secret identity known only to you (and God).

I have plenty of firsthand experience with secret addiction. The seeds that were sown in a cardboard box in the woods at age eleven took root at twenty-two and by thirty-five blossomed into a full-blown addiction to pornography. At this point, in order to be completely honest, I need to make something clear. All porn addictions are actually pornography *and* masturbation addictions. The two go hand-in-hand. No pun intended. Every guy already knows this. So when I say *porn*, understand I mean *P&M*.

(Okay, that was embarrassing. I apologize to our female readers if that grossed you out. I admit there is something repulsive about it. There's a reason people rarely discuss their P&M behavior—when it's exposed it causes incredible shame, and now you know how I feel at this moment. Like I just threw myself under the bus. So be it. I'll go on with my sordid story. Maybe it will help someone.)

Porn addiction is a ball and chain. Neuroscience has demonstrated it has the same effect on the human mind as heroin and is equally difficult to break away from. I believe it. I tried to quit hundreds, maybe thousands of times. My best efforts at applying white-knuckled willpower never lasted more than a couple of weeks.

In the early stages I relied on porn only when I got frustrated. That seemed to work so I started turning to it when I got bored. I got bored A LOT. Eventually I used porn to jumpstart my day. And I'd fall asleep with images of it in my head. I was sneaky and I never got caught.

Day by day I performed my duties as a husband and father to get a handful of red M&Ms. I had lots of friends and they gave me a few more red M&Ms. I'd go to work and get green M&Ms by the ton. But as my dependency on porn grew, my desire for red M&Ms diminished. I grew distant and all of my relationships suffered. Especially my marriage. Poor Rita didn't have a clue what was wrong. As for my relationship with God, the Face of the Father was not even on my radar.

I noticed an ironic twist when I turned forty and began to pursue Amy. My appetite for P&M grew noticeably weaker. Now I know why. She put me back in the hunt for red M&Ms. As we entered into a full-blown affair, my desire for porn dwindled to nothing. I didn't understand why, but being utterly self-deceived, I took it to mean my life was on the right track. We were married eighteen months later. But before the end of our first year of marriage, I was back into porn. By this time the World Wide Web was in high gear and thanks to Internet access I became more hooked than ever. It was like injecting porn into my veins.

At the same time, God was reeling me in. By sheer grace I had brief but compelling glimpses of the Face. I resumed my efforts to battle P&M. But the harder I tried the more I failed.

⌒

One evening I discovered you could surf porn in the comfort of your own home and whenever the wife walked by you could hit one key and all she'd see was email. I went on a porn binge like none I had ever known. I went to bed at midnight that night, satiated but emotionally empty and numb. I woke up an hour later feeling like I had the flu. I headed to the bathroom to hurl. But nothing happened. Then I started shaking uncontrollably and my lower back started aching. That's when I knew I had a kidney stone.

The pain of a kidney stone has been likened to the pain of childbirth without anesthesia. It's true. So I did what most people do when they are in severe pain—I prayed. "Why is this happening to me?" I didn't really have to ask. I already knew. I flashed back to fifth grade and Ricky exclaiming, "They worshiped a dick!" Desperate for relief, I started the bargaining process. "God, if you take this pain away, I will never look at porn again." An hour later I was bundled in blankets on the way to the hospital and convulsing with indescribable pain. As Amy drove, she prayed for me out loud. The instant she said "Amen" the pain stopped. I felt totally normal. Later I was told that the stone must have fallen into my bladder. Maybe that's true, but I know God had everything to do with it.

That experience did a lot to turn me from porn. The way I see it, God used a kidney stone to help set me free. I soon started having more of the Face than ever before. But the porn images were still in my head, competing for the Face. I had cerebral file cabinets full of them. And M sorted through those files on a regular basis and held me captive.

Several months later God intervened on a level much deeper than my urinary tract. I went on a fishing trip to Alaska with my son Dave. But spending quality time with Dave and catching a year's supply of salmon and halibut were not my only goals. I was also on a mission to become free from M. As I sought to hear from God during that trip, a single verse of Scripture landed in my lap like a hot coal. "For the law of the Spirit of life has set you free in Christ Jesus from the law of sin and death."[40] You can distill that down to five little words that became almost audible: *I don't have to sin.* Not when I'm frustrated. Not when I'm bored. This sin wasn't necessary for me to have a good day. I simply do not *have to* do it.

I returned from Alaska knowing I was no longer addicted to P&M. Its power to control me had been broken. You could even say I was delivered. But I see it as being set free from one dependency because a better one had taken its place. This new dependency was what I was made for and I could feel it in every fiber of my being.

This freedom in Christ does not mean I no longer experience temptation. And it doesn't mean I never yield to temptation. It means that when I move down the road toward giving in to temptation there's always a Y in the road. It means there's an alternative direction that is as real and do-able as the road to sin. The signpost reads, *The Way of Escape.*[41] I look up and see it and I can say, "I don't have to do this—instead I will trust him to enable me to take the other path." And when I do, I'm never proud, and always grateful.

⌒

The Way of Escape really helps, but I eventually learned something even more powerful. Something Joe hit on when he said we should remember the cross, and eat. Nearly every morning I spend time alone remembering the cross, meditating on its meaning, and waiting until my heart fills with gratitude. And usually, before too long, as I open the Word and pray over it, my soul is lifted up and I experience the Face of the Father and the transcendent joy that comes with being wrapped in his love. Call it communing with God. Call it fellowship with God. I call it The Morning Feast because I usually come away full and sometimes over-flowing. Those moments under the shadow of the cross, experiencing the Face of God by faith, well, they are exquisite moments.

In the wake of a typical Morning Feast three things are abundantly clear. First, God is infinitely more satisfying than porn or money or any other idol. Second, the thought of feasting on any idol is about as appealing as eating a mouthful of sawdust (or worse). Third, with those sinful desires extinguished and my heart warmed by his Face, I know I am free to love him, worship him, and serve him all day long.

But then I get up from my knees and head out into the cold, cruel world. There's temptation out there, you know? But the deep satisfaction I had in my Morning Feast can carry over. Here's how it works: I know if I give in to temptation my experience of the Face of God will grow dim. But I want the Face more, so I remember the cross, eat a quick Mini-Feast, and place my dependency on him to enable me to enter The Way of Escape.

In the process, most of the time my appetite for sin will weaken and go away. But not always. It's ironic, but if I sin I end up back at the same place—the cross.

126

Do you see how central the cross is to our freedom? At the cross, Jesus frees us from the guilt, condemnation and punishment for our sin. At the cross, he frees us from the power of sin by bringing us to the Father, that we might see his Face. Once again, this is grace flowing from the cross into the cracks of our brokenness.

Do you see? Freedom from addiction is not merely about applying our willpower. It's about feasting on Jesus. How do we do that? It starts with expressing dependence on him and then surrendering to that dependence. Then doing everything that's involved in experiencing your union with him. This leads to adoring him, delighting in him, and enjoying the Face of the Father. God enables this process from beginning to end. By his power, not our willpower, we become free indeed.[42]

11

Garbage Day

JOE

Abraham Maslow is known for his hierarchy of human needs. He theorized that certain needs must be met before others can be addressed. I agree. On mission trips I have noticed a hierarchy of needs: food and water, sleep, and some way to get clean. There are probably better ones but those are mine.

I've been on about three dozen mission trips over the years. Early on, I went on a trip with a small group of high school students. We went to the Dominican Republic just three miles from the Haitian border. I am not a picky eater. I have eaten a gerbil. I thought I would throw that in just in case you doubted the picky eater thing. It tasted a lot like chicken only much smaller. I'm serious. Anyway, on this trip the stuff they fed us was not edible. It was terrible. We slept on cement floors with just sheets between our bodies and the floor. So, two out of three of my deep needs remained unmet. That is when I found out the beauty and wonder of the third need. The one thing we had on this trip was a freshwater spring. Every morning we would get up and stumble down to a pool of water fed by the underground spring. By mid-afternoon the water was murky because it was the only source of water for the village and was used for everything including laundry. But each morning it was brand new. The water was crystal clear and our team would go and wade in the clear cool water. Mango trees hung over the pool and we would throw rocks up to knock down some mangos and we would stand and eat mangos in this water that seemed like it belonged in the garden of Eden. I have never enjoyed mangos as much as I did for those two weeks. Every morning that pool seemed to wash away my need for sleep and good food.

On another trip there was no spring but our team had great food and we had learned to bring air mattresses so the first two needs were met in full. We were mixing concrete and pouring it in hundred-degree heat. Each evening we would walk back to the hull of a building where we had set up camp. We had showers there but we needed electricity to run the pump. For five straight days we walked back, rounded the corner in hopes of seeing the fluorescent lights—our signal that there would be running water—only to be met by darkness. The brownouts that were common in that area kept hitting our compound at just the wrong times. By the fifth day I had built up a layer of sludge on most of my body. It was a weird mixture of sweat, sunscreen, dust, and concrete. My body would itch and every time I would try to scratch, my fingernails would fill with the sludge. We quit changing clothes to go to bed. We would just come home, eat in small dirty huddles, pull off our boots, lie down on our air mattresses, and try to sleep, only to repeat the same thing the next day.

Finally, on the sixth day I had had enough. I talked to one of the locals and found the location of the closest river. After work we walked around the corner and a collective groan went up as we looked at the dark building. I told everyone that I had a surprise for them. We piled into the vans and headed to the river. We got there well after dark. It was actually near an energy plant so we were probably trespassing. I am hoping the statute of limitations has run out. We slowly made our way to the river's edge and waded in just downstream from a breakwater where the water cascaded like a mini waterfall. The feel of the river's current on our legs was exquisite. It is hard to describe unless you have gone without bathing for a long, long time. The grit buildup from working construction in equatorial heat is like dog years to the grit you build up in your normal American day. What I am saying is you would have to go without bathing for months to feel what it was like for us as we entered the rushing water of this blessed river. I squatted down and dunked my head under the surface. There is a type of silence that only happens underwater. It is a stillness and solitude I have always loved. No matter how many people are around above the surface, you are absolutely alone underneath it.

I finally worked my way up to the breakwater and sat down right underneath it. The amount of water flowing over a waterfall is almost always deceiving. The power of the hundreds of gallons cascading onto my head and shoulders was incredible. It was almost frightening. The sensation of every bit of dirt and grit being carried away by the unending flow was indescribable. I sat there for the better part of an hour. My need to become clean was very great.

⌒

Our garbage is picked up on Mondays. I love garbage day. I mean I really love it. Each week I put all our trash out. I separate the plastics and paper to be recycled. Most of the time I am shocked by how much trash has accumulated over a week. I drag it out to the curb before I leave for work. I have one large garbage container and two spare ones for the weeks that are really out of control. Once after a water problem I dragged a whole carpet out there with the pad. As I pulled it down the driveway it left a swath of slime like a giant slug. That carpet was nasty. Anyway, every Monday I pull out all my trash and drive off to work and when I come home later in the day it is gone. I mean all the garbage, no matter how much, no matter how nasty, it is completely gone. I love coming home and seeing the empty trash cans. Most of the time they are left turned upside down just as a sign to me that everything is gone. It has made me love Mondays because garbage day makes me feel clean.

I have a deep need to feel clean. Maybe you do too. I have given two different images because grace hits me both ways. Forgiveness is like garbage day in that no matter what I bring to God it is completely taken away. No matter how much or how nasty, forgiveness is absolutely complete. The cans are turned upside down. But grace is more than that. Grace is also like sitting under the breakwater and having the water cascade over me. It is overwhelming. It is abundant. It is a hair's breadth away from being painful because of its strength. If someone thinks grace is soft it makes me wonder if they have ever really felt it. Grace has never been soft to me.

King David slept with Bathsheba, the wife of Uriah.[43] When Bathsheba became pregnant the King panicked. He ended up setting up Uriah, one of his best friends, to die in battle. When it was over God sent a prophet to confront David about it. David didn't try to spin what he had done. He didn't look at the prophet and bite his lip and say, "I did not have sex with that woman, Mrs. Uriah." David looked down at his shoes and felt the guilt pour over him. It formed a weird sludge, part pride, part lust, part murder, part cover-up. It stuck to his soul like glue. When David wrote Psalm 51, he was longing to be clean. This is what he wrote,

> Have mercy on me, O God, according to your steadfast love; according to your abundant mercy blot out my transgressions.
> Wash me thoroughly from my iniquity, and cleanse me from my sin!

132

For I know my transgressions, and my sin is ever before me.

Against you, you only, have I sinned and done what is evil in
your sight, so that you may be justified in your words and
blameless in your judgment.

Behold, I was brought forth in iniquity, and in sin did my
mother conceive me.

Behold, you delight in truth in the inward being, and you
teach me wisdom in the secret heart.

Purge me with hyssop, and I shall be clean; wash me, and I
shall be whiter than snow.

Let me hear joy and gladness; let the bones that you have
broken rejoice.

Hide your face from my sins, and blot out all my iniquities.

Create in me a clean heart, O God, and renew a right spirit
within me.

David was as dirty as dirty can be. He longed to be made
clean. David didn't need a soft grace. He needed a grace that
was like steel wool. He needed a grace that was stronger than his
sin. There is a breakwater in the Dominican Republic that flows
strong enough to take the grit out from under your fingernails if
you can sit under it long enough. The only thing strong enough
to remove the grit in David's soul or mine flows from a deeper
place. It flows from the veins of God himself. The blood of God
is what has washed my soul.

Forgiveness is like garbage day for me. Whatever I put out there
disappears. But forgiveness is only made possible by grace. The
grace of God is not gentle. It is overwhelming, it is abundant, it
is amazing, but it is not gentle. It flows fast and hard. There is a
power to real grace that is frightening. Grace is not something
that can be walked into gradually. It is not something you can
even wade into. It is something you are plunged into. There is a
silence and solitude when grace really flows. It is the same solitude
and silence I experience when I am underwater. It is the only time
I ever feel completely clean.

As the Poet William Cowper wrote in 1771:

"There is a fountain filled with blood,
    Drawn from Immanuel's veins:
And sinners, plunged beneath that flood,
    Lose all their guilty stains."

BOB

Joe and I have a lot in common. We like a lot of the same things. Sports, mission trips, the ocean, and a good book, to name a few. Today is Wednesday. Garbage day. I just dragged two trash cans out to the street to see if I would get some jollies out of it. I didn't. Joe is weird sometimes. But I'd still take a bullet for him.

I agree with Joe about one thing, though. Grace is not soft. Not at its core. When temptation comes you may hear God's still, small voice whispering, "Remember—you don't have to do it." That part can be kind of soft. But at the core of grace there are only two things. His cross and our brokenness. Neither of those is soft. Neither is easy. But both are essential in order for grace to transform us.

There is a kind of brokenness that's like being pressed up against a wall. Overcome by adverse circumstances, we cry out to God—like Amy and I did with baby Grace in the hospital—because we've exhausted our own resources and there's simply nowhere else to turn. There is also a kind of brokenness that's like wallowing in garbage. Overcome by our own stench we cry out to God as we suffocate in our sin. That was King David in Psalm 51. And that was me at several points in my life. Wallowing in stench is the kind of brokenness I know best. At least so far.

If anybody has been filthy in this world, it's me. The sludge I'm talking about is not under my fingernails. It's on the inside where not even Niagara Falls could wash it away. I'm the kind of person that can make you feel pretty good about yourself by comparison. If I can get clean, anyone can.

So when I tell you that I'm 100 percent clean inside and always will be, you might think I've lost my mind. If you see the gospel as crazy good news you might not see me as a lunatic, but you may still be wondering how I made the journey from point A to point B. From being a guilt-ridden adulterer P&M addict to having rock-solid assurance that all the garbage—past, present, and future—is gone forever, and the waterfall of Living Water has made me, even me, "holy and blameless and above reproach before [God]."[44] The answer is I got a lot of help.

―――――

Seems like everywhere I go these days people want to hear the story of how I hooked up with Jerry Bridges to write books. They recognize the staggering odds against a man of his stature and reputation associating himself as a co-author with a guy like me.

In many circles Jerry Bridges is considered one of the top fifteen living Christian authors. He has something like eighteen titles to his credit, some of which have won awards or become bestsellers. He's best known for *The Pursuit of Holiness*. It came out when I was at Ohio State. I heard about it but I didn't read it. Holiness was not on my radar. I remember thinking that anyone who could write a book with a title like that must be a little scary.

Trust me, Jerry is not scary. He's pretty old, a little hunched over, and he speaks with a soft voice. We met one night eight years ago and something magical started to happen. We began bonding on a deep, spiritual level. Two days later I was asked to take him to the airport. I got an idea for the drive time. I suggested, "How about if you pray and I'm invisible?" Jerry agreed and so he prayed aloud the whole way—about half an hour. His prayer was unforgettable. As his words piled up I could almost see his union with Christ by faith in the gospel. It was that real.

Jerry's flight was delayed so we spent the next hour together in the terminal. I knew I needed a lot of help so I wasted no time telling him my entire life story, including all the gory details. But I lost track of time and left him with a grand total of five minutes to tell me how to fix my life.

Three weeks later I attended a conference where Jerry was speaking. His topic was "The Bookends"—an analogy he uses to describe the way the Christian life works. The first bookend addresses the issue, "How does God accept us?" The second bookend answers, "How do we change?" We spent an hour together afterwards—still not nearly enough time. He told me he would be back in Ohio in a couple months to speak at another conference. He'd have an afternoon off and invited me to spend it with him.

The conference was in Amish country on a beautiful spring day. I showed up with a legal pad loaded with pages of questions. My dilemma could be distilled down to the fact that I had the Face of the Father, but I continued to sin, and the Face would grow dim. Even though adultery and porn addiction were in my past, sin was still present in my life every day. At times I would grieve over my sins to the point of self-loathing. We sat down and I unloaded my questions one by one. Before long I recognized a pattern. I'd ask a question related to the second bookend, how to change. Jerry would give a brief answer and then direct me back to the first bookend, how God accepts us. I'd say something like, "Yes, I know, I get that part." Then I'd ask another question about how to change. And the pattern repeated itself. For three solid hours.

I thanked Jerry and climbed in my pickup truck, a little perplexed. To give myself time to think I took the scenic route home through the heart of Ohio's Amish country. I tried to remember everything Jerry told me, but only one thing stood out. He kept saying, "Never forget—you stand in the present reality of your justification." I knew justification meant *declared righteous*. But I didn't understand how it worked or how it applied to me. Worse yet, I began to wonder if I had ever really experienced what it meant to stand in the *present reality* of it.

I prayed, "Lord, what is this about? Is it for me?" Instantly a verse Jerry shared came to my mind. "He has clothed me with the garments of salvation; he has covered me with the robe of righteousness."[45] All of a sudden I could almost see myself standing before God—completely clothed in pure white from head to toe. The scene seemed to be suspended in time as I gradually became aware that this was a *present* reality. Every part of me—inside and out—was at that very moment covered in White. And the Source of the White was the perfect Son of God and Man who came to fulfill all righteousness—for me! Tears formed in my eyes and silently streamed down my face. I continued driving at full speed even though I could barely see the road. The thought actually crossed my mind that if I crashed into a brick wall I wouldn't even care. I felt lighter than air. I was having the time of my life.

A few days later a letter arrived from Jerry. He recommended two books and an essay—all written over three hundred years ago by authors he affectionately referred to as "the old dead guys." He offered to meet with me after I read it all. I'm a slow reader—I read no faster than you can read aloud. So the task seemed daunting. But almost as soon as I began my eyes were opened to the gospel on a level I never knew existed.

A couple months later I rented a motor home and took Amy, Grace, and Michael out west for a month-long vacation. By this time Grace was five years old and Michael was three. On the third day Jerry and I met in Estes Park, Colorado at the crack of dawn while the family slept. I had a legal pad and pen in hand. Before I could ask my first question, Jerry jumped in and asked me one instead. He asked how I was doing. And I wasn't doing very well. So I dropped my legal pad and told him the truth. I told him I was having difficulty in my marriage. He listened and asked questions and listened some more. He shared from his own life. He gave me advice from the Bible. And he did it with the compassion of a father. We spent a long time in prayer that morning. I can't remember if we ever got around to the legal pad.

The six of us went on an easy hike that afternoon. Jerry and Michael exchanged hats. Michael's looked like a bottle cap on Jerry's head, and Jerry's came down over Michael's ears. By the time we said goodbye my kids were calling him "Uncle Jerry." He's been my mentor ever since. But he became more than a mentor. He became my close friend. I can tell him everything—and I do. And remarkably, he tells me everything too. We share each other's burdens regularly. We pray for each other habitually. And we know each other intimately. The books we have written together have been a byproduct of our relationship. Writing has never been the focus.

⌒

Jerry Bridges understands grace better than anyone I know. I think I know why. He's learned the secret of *staying* broken. He doesn't need a catastrophic circumstance or a collision with repulsive sin in order to keep his dependency locked on Christ. I can see this in his prayer requests. They are often about little things. One time his wife's sewing machine broke. He specifically called to ask me to pray that they could get it fixed in time for her to complete a quilt she had promised someone. That struck me as being a rather small matter. But Jerry is a man who recognizes he's dependent on God for everything all the time. By doing so he abides in a continuous state of brokenness. So grace continuously flows in.

Another way he does this is by being sensitive to his own sin. Here's a little story to illustrate my point. Jerry travels extensively, mostly to speak at conferences. He's over eighty years old and yet each year he spends more days traveling than he does at home. He's on his second million miles of air travel. One day the airlines lost his suitcase. He called me for prayer. He was upset—but not over his lost bag. He was troubled about his sin of anxiety. For failing to trust God about his luggage. That sin may seem like chump change next to yours and mine. But to Jerry this was wallowing in garbage. His sensitivity over his "respectable sins" keeps him in a state of brokenness from day to day. He takes his sin back to the cross where he stands in the present reality of his justification. And grace flows in.

Another way Jerry stays broken is by being humble enough to remain teachable. I sent him an early draft of chapter 10 of this book to get his comments. He offered a suggestion for clarifying the fact that we have to depend on God's enabling power in order to take the Way of Escape. And then he said something that floored me. He told me God used Joe's M&M analogy to show him how to love his wife better. He said, "I need to focus on giving red M&Ms and forget about how many I receive in return. And I need to be reminded that all the green ones belong to Jesus and to him alone. So thank Joe for me." At over eighty years old, Jerry is still learning and growing in grace.

About a year ago Jerry called to tell me about a conflict he ran into with someone. He decided not to be confrontational, but to simply accept the situation. He told me he was going to take a drive and listen to "Blessed Are the Meek," which was one of the messages in his eight-part series on the Beatitudes. I was familiar with this series. He had sent me the CDs and I'd listened to them twice. I decided to take a drive myself and listen to the message Jerry was hearing and try to put myself in his shoes. I jumped in my truck and plugged in my iPod. Within thirty seconds I realized I had never heard "Blessed Are the Meek." I must have skipped over it—twice. The reason I skipped it hit me like a ton of bricks. I wasn't interested in meekness. It didn't appeal to me. Jesus said, "Blessed are the meek," but I wasn't interested in that kind of blessing. As if I knew more about blessing than Jesus did.

It was like that day I drove home through Amish country all over again—only this time I had to pull over because I was bawling like a baby. When I regained a little composure I called Jerry. He was still in his car. I explained what happened. I will never forget what he said. "Everything Jesus did, he did in your place as your substitute. He was patient in your place. He was pure of heart in your place. And he was meek in your place as well." Jerry could not have been more gentle or more kind. And at that moment I was plunged into a raging torrent of grace. I felt crushed. But I felt clean.

Wherever the scuba diving is really good you can usually see groups of tourists waiting their turn to explore the reefs. When they go out, they are always led by a divemaster, someone who has logged a lot of time underwater; an experienced diver who knows how to teach, and how to lead, and who knows the reefs really well. Jerry is like a divemaster in an ocean of grace. He plumbs the depths and wallows in the beauty of the world under the sea. He knows the quiet place of immersion in God's grace very well. And he delights in teaching novices like me to dive deeper.

Oceans are majestic but they are also dangerous. So divers use the buddy system. When the divemaster is your buddy it means you can relax and enjoy the scenery. But it also means you can take on challenges you'd never attempt if your buddy was just another novice. Now you know what my life has been like these past eight years. Beauty and challenge in the ocean of grace with Jerry at my side.

Jerry is a special gift. But I will probably lose him someday. In my mind he's the kind of person who will die in his sleep with a little smile on his face. He will close his eyes and then open them to the beaming Face of the Father. I will be happy for him when the time comes. The trouble with big gifts is they leave big holes when you lose them. But Jerry has taught me by example to treasure the Giver above the gifts—Jesus is the only Treasure I can't live without.

But as far as mentors and friends go, I cannot imagine anyone better than Jerry Bridges. And for that I will be forever grateful.

Tom Randall

12

The Pleasure Spectrum

JOE

The NASCAR parody movie, *Talladega Nights,* has an infamous prayer scene. Ricky Bobby is a successful racecar driver, and in the scene he is saying grace over the take-out from Taco Bell, KFC, and Domino's. During the prayer we learn that he is under contract to mention Powerade every time he prays, but that's not even the strangest part. In his prayer he keeps addressing "baby Jesus." Eventually the prayer is interrupted by a discussion over what God is actually like. Ricky's sidekick Cal steps up and delivers modern theology in a nutshell. He says, "I like to picture Jesus in a tuxedo T-shirt because it says, like, 'I wanna be formal, but I'm here to party, too.' " And by way of explanation he says, "Because *I* like to party, so I like *my Jesus* to party." And there it is. It has always been man's habit to create God in his own image, but it does seem like it is more blatant now than ever.

The combination of creating God in our own image and then seeking his blessing is a fascinating phenomenon. It makes no sense, but we nearly all do it at least once in a while. The more God is like me the more likely we are to see eye to eye on things. Oprah Winfrey believes in God. But the God I've heard her talking about sounds a lot like Oprah. I don't think they ever disagree. Cal would never disagree with a Jesus in a tuxedo T-shirt. They would party side by side, with Jesus carrying the responsibility of keeping the party going.

God, the true God, seems to have made a strategic mistake in creating the capacity for pleasure in the human being. The desire for pleasure is what drives us to create him in our image and seek out blessing at all costs. Oprah's god doesn't disagree with her, because if he did it would limit her pleasure. A God who puts boundaries around sexuality is just unacceptable since sex provides a human being with such exquisite pleasure. A god who would deny a human being that kind of pleasure is a god no one wants.

But pleasure is a little more complicated than most of us realize. For most of us, pleasure seems as simple as choosing between cupcakes and chemotherapy. Cupcakes are good and tasty. Chemo is something no one in their right mind would choose if they didn't have to. So when we are thinking about pleasure, cupcakes win hands down. It is that simple. Or is it?

Years ago I came up with a theory. I call it the Pleasure Spectrum. When God created human beings he gave us a wide range of things that were intended for our pleasure. We have the capacity to get pleasure from viewing a sunset on a cloudless day. We can get goose bumps from listening to the beauty of music. Don't even get me started on taste and touch. Just today I held a bag of freshly ground coffee up close to my face and closed my eyes and inhaled like my life depended on it. The spectrum is very, very wide.

But something interesting happens as we get older. When I was in high school just about any car would give me pleasure. My first car was a wreck that cost me $350. It was a powder blue Plymouth Fury. Now, when I say powder blue I mean it. If you rubbed up against my car you walked away looking a little powder blue yourself. But it ran and that was enough to give me great pleasure. It would not give me the same pleasure today. I have graduated to nicer cars and the Plymouth Fury dropped off the list a long time ago. That means there are fewer cars now that will give me pleasure than there were when I was seventeen. I know people who are wealthy enough that there are only a half dozen cars in the world that will give them pleasure. These same people eat at really nice restaurants. They started eating there on special occasions but then realized they could afford to eat there whenever they went out for dinner. Now when they go out to eat, they have to eat there. Isn't that weird? If you lined up all the restaurants in my town there are some people who could experience great pleasure all the way from Taco Bell to the place with the linen tablecloths and Kobe beef. Other people are limited to the nicest restaurants. There are some people who, out of all those restaurants, can really only go to one and be happy.

Maybe this is obvious by now, but at my church we take a lot of mission trips. One of the side benefits of taking mission trips is that it stretches your pleasure spectrum back out to something more like its original size. After someone gets home from a mission trip every hot shower or cold glass of water is exquisite. It only lasts a little while before the pleasure spectrum begins to close back up, but for a while every mission tripper is happier. It is like a mission-trip aftershock of pleasure.

Every human being if left to himself will slowly but surely begin to narrow the pleasure spectrum. If you have enough money you will begin to shop only at certain stores, drive only certain cars, and eat only at certain restaurants. If you fly in a private jet and the jet is not available one day and you must resort to flying on a commercial jet, you will sit in the big leather chairs in first class. Those of us in coach will shuffle by you to get to our seats. The flight attendant will pull the curtain dividing the two sections. And every person in coach will have a better chance at experiencing pleasure during that flight than you will. All of your hard work and affluence will have left you a tiny sliver of the pleasure spectrum. Perhaps no profession is more dedicated to the pursuit of pleasure than being a rock star. And yet Mick

Jagger screams, "I can't get no satisfaction" right in the middle of satiating himself with everything rock and roll has to offer.

⌒

What if we have the pleasure thing all wrong? What if pleasure is designed to be a side effect? I have a good friend who will say the best year of her life was when she had cancer. She experienced things she had never experienced before. There was a sweetness of relationship, a gratitude for every little thing, and a closeness to God that was unparalleled.

I first met Tom Randall when he was living in the Philippines. Tom has an inviting smile with a gap between his front teeth. He makes me laugh. He makes everyone laugh. I have never met anyone so filled with joy. I have walked with Tom through some deep waters. We narrowly avoided kidnappers in a province just north of Manila. There were three of us and the other guy was a wealthy businessman who loves to build orphanages around the world. I remember thinking as we were trying to out-maneuver the kidnappers that the news summary would read, "Kidnappers hold famous missionary and wealthy businessman for ransom. An unidentified pastor was quickly beheaded to let everyone know they meant business." There is no one I would rather die with than Tom.

Tom had to come back to the States because he was suffering from an overload of toxins in his system after years of riding a motorcycle on the streets of Manila. I was driving with Tom one time near my house when we passed a newly paved section of asphalt. I had to pull over while he threw up just from the smell. If Tom spent too much time in Manila he would develop open sores on the inside of his mouth. I remember walking with him down the streets of Manila and he would lean over and literally blow pus out of his mouth. He couldn't purse his lips to spit. But he never missed a beat. Joy flows out of somewhere deep. Tom's pleasure spectrum is wide open. Everyone who has ever known him would vouch for that. I asked him one time what the secret to his joy was. He said through a toothy grin, "I think it is connected with how much I have suffered." I think that is part of it. There is something about suffering that pulls the pleasure spectrum back out like an accordion. But there is something more.

In the story of the prodigal son both brothers made the same mistake. They went after the Father's stuff but not the Father. The younger son thought the secret to pleasure was pursuing the stuff that gave him pleasure. He ended up in the pig sty feeding the pigs and humming, "I can't get no satisfaction." The pursuit of pleasure is always a losing battle especially if you catch it. The older brother wanted to experience what the younger brother experienced. But he didn't get to and ended up sulking outside the party. The key for both of them was right there inside the house. It was the father himself.

God has made you for himself. Pleasure was only created as a gift of love from God. The experience of pleasure was designed to communicate the love of God. When we split pleasure off from the love of God it is cut off from the life source and thrashes around for a while before it lies there motionless and dead.

I have watched Tom laugh until the tears roll down his cheeks while he's lying on the floor of a hut in the middle of a jungle. I have heard him laugh on the phone as he tells me about playing golf at Pebble Beach with his new friend Tom Watson. Nearly every time I talk to Tom I ask him how he is doing. His answer is always the same. He says, "Joe, I am having the time of my life." And then he laughs long enough to make me smile and laugh with him. Tom travels with the Father. That is the secret. Everywhere Tom goes he is experiencing the love of the Father and as far as I can tell the Father loves to travel with Tom.

God made you to experience exquisite pleasure for all of eternity. Heaven is full of all the Father's stuff, but the thing that makes it heaven is the presence of the Father. A place that would have all the Father's stuff without the Father would soon become hell.

BOB

In *Blue Like Jazz*, Donald Miller tells a story he says is "as accurate a description of hell as can be calculated."[46] He could be right, even though most of the story is a cartoon. The images stuck in my mind, and took the meaning of the word *horror* to a new level.

In case you don't already have his book, let me summarize the story for you. Don Astronaut works on a space station. He wears a special spacesuit that can sustain his life indefinitely. One day there's an explosion that sets him adrift. As he floats in space, all his bodily functions are perfectly supported by the suit. Months go by and he loses all hope of being rescued. Meanwhile his hair grows long and his beard grows shaggy. It's a problem the spacesuit designers apparently didn't anticipate. Years pass and hair has nearly filled his helmet, covering his eyes so he can barely see. It even grows into his mouth and up his nostrils. Don Astronaut is absolutely alone, cut off from everything and everybody, including God, floating aimlessly in space, every day a little more blinded and a little more choked by hair that never stops growing. If you seriously try to imagine an endless existence like that, I guarantee you will shudder at the core of your being. It would be hell.

I attended my first funeral at the beginning of third grade. I stood in a line with my parents watching each person take their turn kneeling in front of Great-Grandma's open casket. Almost everyone kissed the corpse—usually on the forehead, but sometimes on the lips. My turn came and I knelt there alone, gawking. Her face looked like modeling clay coated with powder make-up. That was disturbing, but the sight of her line-thin grayish lips made me cringe. There'd be no kissing, that was for sure. Just when I thought I'd put in enough time, the unthinkable happened. Her hand twitched. I kid you not. And a half-hour later I watched them close the casket on her and latch it shut.

I didn't tell anyone about the experience until years later when I took Human Cadaver Lab at Ohio State. In the orientation session we were told that body parts sometimes quiver because of biochemical reactions that occur inside decaying muscle tissue. I raised my hand and unloaded my funeral story for the first time. When I got to the part about my recurring nightmares of being buried alive, the lab instructor interrupted me. "Save it for psych class." Everyone laughed, but I thought he was somewhat insensitive. By the way, before the course was over I saw one dead guy's face flinch and another one's arm quiver and it still gave me the willies.

Twenty-five years later I was investing in outpatient imaging centers. One day, technicians were installing an MRI and needed a human guinea pig for a test run. I volunteered because I had a crick in my neck and hoped they would diagnose it.

It was not an open MRI. That means they lay you on a motorized table face-up and slide your entire body headfirst into a tube that's so narrow your shoulders touch it on either side. There's only six inches of clearance in front of your face. After about ten seconds I felt like I was going to freak out. And before I knew it I was thrashing around uncontrollably, screaming at the top of my lungs, "Get me outta here!" It took forever for the motorized table to slide me out of that thing. When my head finally cleared the tube, I bolted upright and saw a half-dozen people staring at me in silence. I felt like a complete idiot. I apologized, left that place, and never went back.

That night I crawled into bed and fell asleep. I was exhausted. Two hours later a sense of absolute panic jolted me awake. It took three miserable hours for me to calm down enough to get back to sleep. This happened every night for a week before I finally connected the dots to the MRI fiasco, my great-grandma, and the recurrent nightmares of my childhood. I got a prescription for some high-power sleeping pills and knocked myself out each of the next several nights. I still keep the pills around, just in case.

Now you know why the images of Don Astronaut are stuck in my mind. Eternal conscious aloneness in utter darkness—that would be hell for anyone. Especially me.

147

I've thought a lot about James 1:17. It's basically an encouraging verse but it's also scary if you consider the implications. Read it slowly: "Every good gift and every perfect gift is from above, coming down from the Father of lights with whom there is no variation or shadow due to change." Now ask yourself, "What if I were totally cut off from God?" If *every* good thing comes from God as its source, then if you were cut off from God there would be zero good things. None. So I guess James 1:17 means hell won't have any of God's stuff. At least not his good stuff. If that's true then hell, at best, would be a lot like being buried alive. The big difference being that it's not just a nightmarish dream, so you can't wake up from it. And there are no pills to make it go away. You're stuck with it forever.

We get some more insight into hell from Jesus' parable about two men who at first are on opposite ends of the pleasure spectrum—a rich man who is unnamed, and a dirt-poor beggar named Lazarus.[47] The story opens with the rich man living the height of the good life. Meanwhile, Lazarus begs for a measly crumb to eat—a pretty broad pleasure spectrum there—while dogs lick the open sores that cover his body. The rich man sees all this, rolls his eyes, yawns, and takes an afternoon nap on a pile of silk cushions.

Lazarus dies and angels escort him to heaven where he becomes bosom buddies with Father Abraham. The rich man eventually dies, too. He shows up in hell where, as Jesus puts it, he is "in torment." The rich man now has the huge pleasure spectrum that Lazarus once had—he begs for a single drop of water "to cool my tongue, for I am in anguish in this flame." So, according to Jesus, hell is worse than being Don Astronaut or being buried alive. Not only is there no good stuff in Hades, like a drop of water, but there's seriously bad stuff, like flame that causes anguish.

Okay, I don't really know what hell is like—I'm only speculating based on Don Miller, James, and Jesus. But I know a place where we can look behind hell's curtain if we dare. It's at the cross. What do we see there? Darkness? Yes. Torment? Yes. Anguish? Yes, of course. Separation from all mankind? Yes. Separation from God? Yes. That's why Jesus screamed at the top of his lungs, "Eloi, Eloi, lema sabachthani"[48] in a way that made gnashing of teeth seem like child's play. Remember, until the cross, Jesus had been infinitely inseparable from the Father. The two had been perfectly one.[49] So on the cross, the extent of agony caused by even temporary alienation and isolation from the Father, is immeasurable—far more than all of us put together would experience during an eternity in hell. Jesus experienced hell for us so that we could have heaven. And that's something a Jesus in a tuxedo T-shirt could never do.

⌒

I have a friend who has taken the art of "creating God in our own image" to the next level—he creates heaven in his own image, too. George believes heaven is precisely whatever you think it is. If you think heaven is a beautiful golf course, then for you that's what heaven will be. As if by virtue of you thinking it up, it actually *becomes* your conscious reality when you die. So if you think heaven is an eternal day at the beach, or seventy-two virgins or Chippendales, or a fountain flowing with Patrón tequila, then that's what you get when you arrive. You can even change channels when you get bored. George would tell you, "Scientists agree that 80 percent of the human mind is not engaged in our day-to-day activities. Why? Because that's the brainpower we use to create and maintain our own individual heaven."

What if George is right about heaven, but the real God isn't there? According to Joe even this would soon become hell. A really nice hell, but hell nonetheless. So if George's heaven is not the real heaven, what is?

I figured the apostle Paul should have some answers, seeing that he had been "caught up into the third heaven." I looked up that passage and it turns out he threw in the towel when it came to putting that particular experience into words.[50] But other passages indicate Paul clearly believed that in heaven we'll have our same individual identity—I'll still be me and you'll still be you. And he believed our bodies will be like the resurrected body of Jesus. He wrote this amazing sentence, "Our citizenship is in heaven, and from it we await a Savior, the Lord Jesus Christ, who will transform our lowly body to be like his glorious body, by the power that enables him even to subject all things to himself."[51]

That's powerful stuff, but Paul left a lot of my questions about heaven unanswered, so I kept looking. And it's ironic—a guy who is most famous for his sermon about hell helped me the most to find some words to describe heaven.[52] Jonathan Edwards, according to a Wikipedia entry I read, "is widely acknowledged to be America's most important and original philosophical theologian, and one of America's greatest intellectuals." Edwards died in 1756, but before he did he wrote some amazing words like these about the pleasures of heaven:

"To go to heaven, fully to enjoy God, is infinitely better than the most pleasant accommodations here. Fathers and mothers, husbands, wives, or children, or the company of earthly friends, are but shadows; God is the substance. These are but scattered beams; God is the sun. These are but streams; God is the ocean."

Cool. But don't you wonder sometimes? What could possibly be so great about a place where our focus is on just one thing all the time? Even if that one thing is God. Wouldn't it get really old after a while? Edwards had a great four-point answer to that question. Here's my paraphrase:

1. God is infinite. We are finite. Furthermore, God will always be infinite and we will always be finite.
2. Therefore we can never know everything there is to know about God. In heaven, there will be a fresh new discovery about him around every corner.

3. Link that truth with this one: In heaven our joy is directly proportional to our knowledge of the triune God.
4. Therefore it must follow that throughout eternity our joy will perpetually expand and intensify as we get to know God more and more. And that will be anything but boring.

David, the psalmist, tells us that in God's presence there is "fullness of joy" and at his right hand there are "pleasures forevermore."[53] Whoa! Eternal *pleasures*? I think if Edwards were sitting around in his powdered wig reading this chapter he'd raise a bony finger and say, "See? The Pleasure Spectrums for people in heaven and hell are the same—they are both wide-open, but for opposite reasons. In hell it's the absence of the Father. In heaven it's the presence of the Father. In heaven—the more pleasure you receive, the more pleasure you are capable of receiving. The triune God is there, Father, Son and Holy Spirit, so the potential for experiencing new pleasures is never-ending!"

Edwards predicted that in heaven there will be new kinds of physical matter and even new dimensions that will take our ability to experience pleasure to new heights. He wrote:

"God can contrive matter so that there shall be other sorts of proportions that may be quite of a different kind, and may raise another sort of pleasure in [our senses], and, in a manner inconceivable to us in the here-and-now, shall be vastly more ravishing and exquisite."

And not only that. According to Edwards, in heaven "every perceptive faculty shall be an inlet of delight." That means all our senses will be enhanced and fine-tuned to maximize our enjoyment. I think Paul would have agreed. He wrote, "No eye has seen, nor ear heard, nor the heart of man imagined, what God has prepared for those who love him."[54] In other words, the sights and sounds that await us in heaven are beyond our wildest, most pleasurable dreams.

Edwards described heaven as a place where our hearts and minds will be stimulated in such ways as to "cause a sweet sensation throughout the body, infinitely excelling any sensual pleasure on earth." Hmm. I read that to Amy and she blushed. He's talking about transcendent, God-centered, bodily, sensual pleasure. And just think—that idea came from the mind and quill of a Puritan.

Here's another insight from the psalmist: "Delight yourself in the Lord, and he will give you the desires of your heart."[55] I think it's safe to say that everyone in heaven will truly delight in God. And as we delight ourselves in him, our desire for him will increase. And he delights to satisfy our desires for him in unspeakably pleasurable ways that will delight us with him even more, increasing our desire for him, which he again satisfies, and on and on. That's why heaven is an upward spiral of desire and delight that never ends.

That's great, but what about now? I got to thinking about Tom Randall and Rob Thomas. It seems like most of their pleasures on earth have been the God-centered kind, driven by a Christ-focused delight and desire. If so, no wonder Rob is always wigging out and Tom is always having the time of his life—their lives are, to a large degree, heaven on earth. I've had some pleasures like that over the past fourteen years. When I hold the memories of those exquisite moments in my mind and examine them closely, something becomes clear. Every one of those moments glorified God. I think that's what heaven will be like—we get the pleasure and God gets the glory. Every time. And it just keeps on getting better and better.

If you understand the gospel you know there could be no heaven for us if there had been no hell for Jesus on the cross. It's ironic to think that the place where we see ultimate hell is the same place where we see ultimate love. It's the place where heaven's door opens to sinners like Tom, Rob, Joe, Amy, me, and you.

Amy and Rita

13

Liquid Grace

JOE

Grace is more of a liquid than a solid. I think most of us know that implicitly which is why we say that grace flows. Solids are more passive. You can put something solid on a table and it will just sit there until you come back and move it. But a liquid is different. A liquid needs to be contained or it will run all over the place. Liquids are not passive. I had a small leak in a pipe in the upstairs of my house. Water made it all the way to the basement and by the time I noticed anything it was emerging in multiple places. In fact, there was no telling where the water had gone or what paths it had taken. If there was even the tiniest opening the water slid through and kept going. Such is the nature of liquid. Grace is more liquid than solid. Once it is unleashed there is no telling how far it will go or where it will end up.

I worked at a Christian school for several years after my little brother John died. I was mad at God and a pastor who is mad at God is just not real effective. So after I was asked to leave the church I was serving, I took a job teaching Bible at a Christian school. It was a great time of healing for me. A Christian institution is a very tough animal, especially a Christian high school.

153

The Christian faith is founded upon grace and yet you cannot run a school on grace. Our school had a dress code which started us off in a hole simply because it gave the distinct impression that Christianity, at least our brand, was all about rules. Anyway, it was an independent school, which means the faculty was a pretty good mix of people from different backgrounds and different theological persuasions. I taught Bible and was the chaplain of the school. I spent my days teaching classes and meeting with students. One of my fellow teachers was a very conservative lady who was a strict Baptist. She was the kind of person you would expect to be teaching at a Christian school in the Midwest. Mrs. E was about as tightly wound as they come. She was not a favorite among students. She was a stickler for all things legalistic.

Tracy came to our school as a sophomore. Her hair was bleached white. Our school would take on a certain number of projects each year. Tracy was a project. She came from a troubled home and she had absorbed enough to be trouble herself by the time she arrived. Tracy was tough. For our school she was just scary. Tracy gave the impression she would be much more at ease on a bar stool with a cigarette in one hand and swirling a drink in another than in a Bible class. She was always on the verge of being kicked out. We became friends partly because she spent a lot of time in my office.

About two months into her senior year we were in my office chatting. She sat leaning back in a chair with her legs crossed and her bleached hair disheveled. She was only missing the cigarette and the drink. I hadn't talked with her for weeks so we were catching up. She happened to mention she was a student assistant. That surprised me because student assistants were volunteers who helped teachers. The job was usually reserved for model students and teachers' pets. Besides, I couldn't imagine which teacher Tracy would want to assist. I said, "Really! No kidding. Tracy, what teacher are you the student assistant for?" I didn't even try to hide my surprise. Tracy was a good reader of people and it was better not to try to fake anything with her. She said,

"Mrs. E." I was dumbfounded. Mrs. E would have been one of the last people I would have picked. I said, "Seriously? I have to tell you, I did not see that coming." Tracy laughed and said, "Yeah, I know." If she had had a cigarette that's when she would have taken a long draw and then done one of those exhales where nothing comes out at first and then a stream of smoke that seems like it will never end.

This is what Tracy told me. She said, "Pastor Joe, I hated Mrs. E. I mean I really hated her. I had her for class last year and I worked her—and there was not a day that went by where I didn't let her know how much I detested her. Just before Thanksgiving I had a big fight with my mom. She kicked me out. I called my dad but he didn't want me either. When Mrs. E found out I had nowhere to go for Thanksgiving she invited me to her house." Tracy quit looking out the window and looked straight at me. Then she said, "I didn't go but I have loved her ever since." Grace. Tracy was tough and she was hard. But when Thanksgiving hit her with enough force, a crack appeared that ran from head to toe. Out of nowhere, Mrs. E. poured grace and it ran all over Tracy until it made its way right to her heart.

⌒

I have known Noel for several years. He is mostly Lebanese, which makes him a very pleasant shade of brown. He shaves his head and has a smile that wrinkles up his eyes. His voice is gentle and soft like warm water so all in all my friend Noel is like a human pillow walking around. He just makes people feel at ease around him. We started something at our church a couple of years ago. During the month of December we try to blanket our area with five thousand acts of random generosity. We do it to remind people of what Christmas is all about. The stories that come back are amazing. Our people have done everything from buying a cup of coffee for someone to paying a mortgage payment for a perfect stranger. We have cards printed up that say simply, "You've Been Gifted." The idea is to do something surprisingly generous and then hand the person the card, say "Merry Christmas" and walk away. I have one guy from my church who went to the Goodwill store and just started going crazy stepping in front of people and buying their stuff. It was like a party. He had so much fun he went back the next day and when the cashiers saw him they broke out in applause. Cool.

But back to Noel. Noel went to Walmart and prayed that God would lead him to the right person to gift. He got in a checkout line behind a woman in a wheelchair and her adult daughter. They were trying to pay for their purchases but their credit cards were not going through. Noel saw the opening, stepped up and said, "Hey, why don't you let me buy that for you today?" The checkout clerk said, "You can't do that." Noel smiled and crinkled his eyes and said gently, "Why?" The clerk turned the monitor to show him the total was $192. Noel said, "That's okay. Our church has challenged us to look for ways to be generous and gift people so this is my time. Ladies, please let me be the one that gifts you today." The woman in the wheelchair began to cry. Noel told me later she began to sob. She reached up and took Noel's face in her hands. He didn't even have to smile. She crinkled his eyes for him. She held his face close and said, "I didn't think kindness like this still existed." Then she told him the reason she was shopping that day was for her husband's funeral. At that news, the cashier threw her hands in the air and said, "Praise God" and then asked Noel where he went to church because she wanted to go to a church where people were as nice as he. Noel said it was becoming a scene and he started to panic. He told me he started to babble phrases like, "It's okay. It's no big deal" and "I have a lot of money." Grace. In the middle of Walmart my friend Noel unleashed grace, and grace flowed into the cracks of a broken heart as it is always prone to do.

I met Todd on a Saturday night at church, but we became friends on the bike path. Todd had moved to Ohio from California and had picked up cycling to try to fill the hole where surfing had been. He told me his story as we sat nose-to-nose at Starbucks huddled at one of their undersized tables. Todd had been a youth pastor and then a church planter. The youth pastor thing came easy to him but the church planter gig wiped him out. Ministry can wear people thin as tissue and Todd got so thin he began to tear at the edges. He ended up a customer in a sleazy massage parlor. It took him three years to tell his wife about it and when he did it took her about three minutes to pack her stuff. A minister who wears thin and then tears loses just about everything. If you are a banker you may lose your wife but you go to work the next day and life goes on. Not so with a minister. Todd's wife moved back home to Ohio with their daughter and Todd just staggered around in SoCal for a few months. He finally packed up and moved to Ohio just to be close to his daughter and try to find some healing.

It has been a little over a year since I heard that story. Last week I sat with Todd at the same Starbucks. He told me he had made peace with his wife and felt some healing with his daughter. He said it was time for him to go back to California. We sat and talked about life and about Jesus. He thanked me for being his friend. He was just beginning to open up to the possibility of dating again. He said he had told his story to a young woman a few weeks earlier. It was pretty much the same story he told me. After he finished telling her, she sat quiet for a minute. Todd waited and looked at his shoes. She finally looked at him and said, "I think it takes great courage to be honest. Thank you for trusting me with your story. I think you are a beautiful person." Tears squirted from his eyes as he recounted to me what she had said to him. He said, "Joe, she was so gracious. What do I do with that?" Grace came into my tissue-thin friend and it went so deep he didn't know how to respond.

Grace is not solid, it is liquid. It flows. But grace does need one thing. It needs cracks. The bigger the crack, the deeper grace will penetrate. A soul with no cracks is like a piece of marble. Grace just runs off but never gets in. Tracy cracked when she had nowhere to go for Thanksgiving. At Walmart, Noel found a woman whose husband had just died. After losing all he ever held dear, Todd felt grace flowing back. Cracks and grace go together. When grace does find a crack to move into there is no telling how far it will go and what it will end up doing. Such is the nature of grace.

BOB

One thing I've learned from writing this book is that everybody has stories. You probably have many that should go into a book. And we all have a few stories that are so good it seems like they can't be true. This is one of those stories. When I tell you about how my former wife, Rita, was transformed by grace in the decade after our divorce, you're probably going to think I made it up.

After our divorce was finalized in July 1997, things went from bad to worse for Rita. It started when she found out Amy and I were getting married near a beautiful waterfall in the Cuyahoga Valley National Park—and the wedding party consisted of Dave and Lauren. Rita used to kid me that when she turned forty, I would trade her in for two twenty-year-olds. That was supposed to be a joke. Amy was twenty-five. The next month Rita sold the house—an authentic English Tudor built in the 1920s. It had ivy-covered walls and a slate roof and giant oak trees all around. It was Rita's dream home. She moved from there into a two-bedroom condo. Three months after that upheaval, right before her first Christmas as a single mom, Rita was diagnosed with stage IV breast cancer. That meant radical mastectomy, twenty-two aggressive chemotherapy treatments, and an incalculable number of vomiting episodes. She lost all her hair and wore a baseball cap because the wig just wasn't getting it. And she dwindled to less than a hundred pounds.

Rita has always been a little feisty. She had a tough childhood. Her dad died of lung cancer when she was two, leaving the family destitute and living in the projects. Her mother remained single, pulled herself up by her bootstraps, put herself through college, and eventually became a speech pathologist. But in the process she was seldom very nurturing to Rita. In 1998, Rita was too weak to be feisty. Given all she was dealing with, it's totally understandable that anger would sometimes erupt through her pain.

For example, Rita made it abundantly clear to me that her cancer was my fault. An army of people from her school had affirmed this. To them I was guilty of adultery *and* attempted murder. To this day I sometimes wonder if they were right.

Thankfully, to everyone's surprise, by the end of 1997, Rita's cancer treatment appeared to be successful. Her immune system recovered to the point where she was eventually able to leave the condo without much risk of infection. But her car needed some extensive repairs. I offered to pay for them and to let her drive one of my cars in the meantime. She let me know in no uncertain terms not to bring "her" car. Rita literally couldn't get the name "Amy" on her lips. She told me the thought of touching Amy's steering wheel was repulsive. "Like getting cooties?" I asked. "Yeah," she replied, "like cooties, only worse."

As Rita continued to recover and grow stronger, so did her anger. It usually took the form of sarcasm. She targeted our newfound faith most of all. Any suggestion that people like Amy and me could find forgiveness at the cross made her want to puke.

When Lauren reached the age where she could decide for herself which parent to live with, she decided to move in with me. Rita showed up unexpectedly to have a little chat with Amy about it. It got ugly. I can't repeat what she said. This is a PG-13 book. Life went on like that for almost seven years. In other words, everything about our divorce up to that point was pretty much normal.

Amy and I went to Colorado Springs for a marriage retreat in February 2004. We learned about the Five Love Languages, five ways people give and receive love. The second night I got a phone call from Rita's brother. He told me Rita was in the hospital. And she wasn't expected to live. She had suffered a bowel obstruction and 90 percent of her small intestine had been removed because gangrene had set in. They did not sew her back up. Instead, they sprinkled antibiotic powder into her abdomen and covered it with something like Saran Wrap. If the infection got into her bloodstream she would die. He said I better get back to be there for our kids. Just in case.

We caught a red-eye home and I headed straight to the hospital. I found my way to the surgical waiting room. Dave and Lauren were crying. Rita's mother and brother were there, too. They were too worried and sad to be angry with me. They actually asked me to say a prayer. So I did.

Rita's life hung in the balance for several days. But she survived and eventually returned home to the condo. Recovering from abdominal surgery is always difficult. But getting what remained of her gastro-intestinal system working again was a major challenge. She came very close to needing a permanent feeding tube.

Six weeks later Rita was finally well enough to leave the condo. But she couldn't drive because her car was a stick shift and working a clutch was out of the question. She needed to trade cars for a couple months with someone with an automatic transmission. Those were back in my BMW days, so my car was no help. I was surprised when Rita asked me if I thought Amy would trade cars with her. Amy was surprised too. Shocked. But Amy immediately agreed.

Rita returned Amy's car two months later. It was as shiny as the day we bought it. On the passenger seat was a gift-wrapped box. One of the Five Love Languages is "gifts," and I knew that was Rita's language. I told that to Amy and the gift became deeply meaningful. Seven years have passed and Amy still keeps that gift in her purse and the card in her jewelry box. It marked a turning point. A trickle of grace into a crack.

Before long Rita was struggling financially. Her disability insurance didn't pay a dime for six months. All her money was tied up in her condo and retirement accounts. I was paying child support, but that was all because I had pre-paid everything else when the divorce was finalized. The child support wasn't going to keep Rita's head above water. One day I started to tell this to Amy. She stopped me mid-sentence. I figured she didn't want to hear about it. Instead, she said, "We ruined Rita's life. The least we can do is give her some money." So we did. And a brand new car, too. We were catching on to the love language thing.

Dave graduated from high school later that year. Rita didn't feel up to having a separate graduation party for her side of the family. She asked me to have a combined party at our place. By now Amy and I were living in *my* dream house. It was a log cabin that looked more like a ski lodge. I agreed to host the party even though I was worried her relatives would be steamed just seeing where I lived.

Everyone was a little on edge at first. Rita arrived early and four-year-old Grace ran up to greet her. I overheard the introduction. Rita introduced herself to Grace as Rita. I guess she thought calling herself Mrs. Bevington would be confusing. Anyway, the guests started to arrive and within a half-hour the mood was almost festive. Grace followed Rita like a little shadow. It soon became obvious to everyone that Rita and Grace were enjoying each other. Halfway through the party I noticed something even more astonishing. There was absolutely no tension in the air. Eventually everyone noticed and wondered how that could be.

Three months later we had a birthday party for Dave. We invited Rita. The scene at the dinner table was surreal. Rita sat next to Amy and told stories about Dave's childhood. Everyone laughed until their sides hurt. After the meal Grace sat on Rita's lap and the stories continued. No one wanted to leave. Late that night, as Rita walked to her car, I asked her how that evening could have happened. She simply said, "It's grace."

Rita's health eventually improved. She moved to Boca Raton to take a teaching job since Lauren had enrolled at nearby Palm Beach Atlantic University. When Rita found out about my plans to bring the family to visit Lauren, she invited us to stay at her place. It was a small apartment. That meant Rita would stay with a friend, Grace and Michael would sleep in the living room, and Amy and I would sleep in Rita's bed. I guess cooties were a thing of the past.

Fast-forward four years. Lauren was getting married. Rita came up from Florida and stayed at our place for a month to help with the wedding preparations. By then my dream house and BMW phase was over. We live in an average-sized home for our community. A vinyl-sided Colonial. That means the guest room is about twelve feet from the master bedroom. But there was no tension, no stress and no awkwardness.

Even though it was obvious Rita had already forgiven us, Amy felt like she should ask Rita for forgiveness anyway. She waited for a quiet moment and then pulled Rita aside. It turned into a three-hour conversation. A deep bond formed between them that day, a true friendship—one that has continued to grow to this very day.

We had a lot of laughs as Lauren's wedding day approached. Dinnertime was special every night. The wedding would be a big one—over three hundred guests and thirty people in the wedding party. After the rehearsal dinner, all the bridesmaids and a few groomsmen headed to the church to decorate the fellowship hall for the reception. As they left the church at midnight one of the bridesmaids discovered she had locked her keys in her car. So she called the police. Rita, Amy, and a couple of groomsmen waited with her in the church parking lot. Amy turned on her car stereo and opened all the doors. Before long they were jamming to "Funky Town." Rita and Amy were especially animated and in the zone. When the police arrived the two of them didn't notice and just kept on boogying. The cops asked if Rita and Amy were drunk. But they hadn't had a drop to drink. The bridesmaid, who now had her car keys back, offered a possible explanation, "I guess they're just enjoying the moment?" She was right. The next day the wedding was beautiful. It was perfect. The after-party continued at our home until 4 a.m. Nobody wanted it to end. And Rita stayed an extra week.

I co-teach an eight-week course at Christ Community Chapel called Oasis. It's for people who are going through marriage conflict or divorce recovery. Rita was still in town when the final session came around so I asked her to lead it. She agreed and word got around that she was speaking. We were already an anomaly at CCC—picture the three of us sitting together for Sunday worship. So when the time came for the Oasis class it was standing room only. Amy, Dave, and Lauren were there, too.

Rita began by telling the story of our divorce, losing her dream home, her bout with cancer, the near-death experience of her bowel obstruction, and the emotional suffering she endured through it all. Then she paused. It was a long pause. Then she said something no one in that room will ever forget. "The turning point for me happened when I came to the realization that pain was not the enemy. Sin was." Here's the surprising part—she never mentioned my sin or Amy's. She was talking about her own sin. She got specific about it, too. She described her sin as the way she had tried to control everything in her life. And the way she had depended on everything except God. She talked about how God had used all the brokenness to draw her closer to himself and to enable her to shift her dependence onto him. She said that when she finally recognized how much God had forgiven her because of Jesus, she became free to forgive Amy and me from the heart. At that point you could hear a pin drop. Rita finished by playing a Don Henley song called "Heart of the Matter" while Dave, Lauren, Amy and I shared a group hug with her. Forgiveness, even if you don't love me anymore.

There was not a dry eye in the room. Since that day Rita has been a permanent part of the Oasis ministry at our church.

―――

A year later Amy asked me to buy her a ticket to fly to Florida to spend a week with her special friend. So I did. I got to be Mr. Mom and it was cool because I got our kids to do chores. That's also the week I wrote my half of chapter 5 where I talk about my lies, affair and divorce. I emailed it to Rita to make sure she was okay with it. She called me an hour later and told me about the long talk she and Amy had on the beach that afternoon. Rita had described to Amy many of the painful details of what she went through. They cried together. And they laughed together, too. But mostly they delighted in the discovery that the healing was as deep as the ocean in front of them. "Actually," she told me, "I found what you wrote in that chapter to be comforting in a strange way." She said it was an affirmation that the marriage was real at one time, and that it wasn't all a waste.

By definition, grace means we are not deserving. All three of us know this—we've done nothing to deserve the kind of healing we've experienced. We've simply received grace from God through Christ, and then we've watched it flow in and around and through and between the three of us. Grace has filled the biggest cracks in our lives. It looks weird to some. But to us it's nothing less than wonderful evidence that the gospel can change anything. ANYTHING!

Joe invited Amy and I to join Karen and him and eighteen other couples on a trip to Israel for a tour of the Holy Land. As I write this it's coming up soon. We'll be away from Grace and Michael for almost two weeks. Amy told me there was only one person in the world she would want to be in our home taking care of our kids for that length of time. Guess who it is? You'll find out in chapter 16.

Pastor Marshall Brandon

14

Incarnation

Give Up, Go To, Be With

JOE

She lived one street over and had crossed through the little patch of woods between our houses. It had been raining for three days so the yard was one part grass and three parts mud. With the woods as a barrier, we had never spoken, but I guess she knew I was a minister. When I answered the knock at the back door her eyes looked sad and a little desperate. Her husband was dying, she said, and she wanted someone to pray with him. I put on my shoes and we walked in muddy silence to her house. Her husband lay in a hospital bed in the middle of the living room dying of liver cancer. His skin was greenish gray yet he looked monochrome against the white hospital sheets. He couldn't speak. I'm not even sure he knew I was there. I sat for a while. I held his hand and prayed for him. His wife thanked me and I mumbled some words, hoping to comfort her.

I walked back to my house and the man died that night. I don't know if I helped anyone. But I knew I had been called to the most ancient and powerful movement of the Christian faith.

Give up, Go to, Be with. It is the movement of the incarnation. The muddy footprints I made had been made before by God himself. It was God I was imitating whether I realized it or not, and that made the walk itself holy. The incarnation is as holy a movement as has ever been.

There is something inside of every human being that wants to be the center. We want to be the one who is served. I was reading about Galileo not too long ago and the trouble he had convincing the scientific and religious communities that the earth was not the center of the universe. Everyone was so sure that everything else had to revolve around us. It is always hard to believe our lives are not the most important thing happening at any given moment. It is almost impossible to get out of our skin and really see someone else fully and completely. Maybe when God made the earth revolve around the sun he was trying to tell us something. Maybe he was preparing us for a little disappointment.

So while there is something inside us that wants to be the center of the universe there is something deeper still that comes alive when we enter the movement of Christ to give up, go to, and be with.

One summer, on another trip to the Dominican Republic, I took seventy seventeen-year-olds to work on an orphanage. The building needed a new concrete roof, and since the concrete had to be mixed on the ground and hoisted up by hand, a big crew was a must. You may be aware that high-school juniors are not generally known for their philanthropy. There are few other times in a life when the world is smaller or more intense than when you're seventeen. But this was a chance to get away from their parents and it looked like an adventure so they signed up, went through the training, and joined me for two weeks of backbreaking labor in the relentless Caribbean heat.

Most of those two weeks we spent preparing for The Big Pour. We cut molds and wired rebar until our hands were raw. Finally the day came. Supplies arrived in stages so it was 1:00 p.m., the hottest part of the day, before we could begin. For the next eleven hours we mixed and hauled concrete. The kids tag-teamed with shovels and buckets. At six o'clock some Dominican women brought pots of spaghetti. Girls dished out spaghetti to guys who ate standing up, waiting for their partners to yell for relief. Concrete spattered everyone and everywhere. The sun set, trading scorching heat for stifling heat plus mosquitoes, and still we worked. At midnight we hauled the last bucket to the roof. In eleven hours we had mixed, hauled, hoisted, and poured one hundred tons of concrete. I had never seen teenagers work so hard for so long.

We huddled together smiling and laughing. We prayed and then headed to the river to wash off the chunks of concrete that had become one with our skin. We sang while we walked the kilometer to the river's edge. Every kid on that trip remembers it to this day. I still have young men and women come up to me from that trip and when they talk about The Big Pour their faces light up. It is not pride that fills them. It is the feeling of incarnation. It is the conviction that for eleven hours they were doing something they were absolutely meant to do. It was breathtaking to be so much like God if only for half a day.

⌒

Walk into any Baptist church and ask why Jesus came to earth and they can tell you. He came to die on the cross to pay for your sins. He did it to save your soul. But what does that actually mean and how does it impact the way you live? Your soul is that thing inside your body that gives it the spark of life. When God kneeled over Adam while Adam was still just a Play-Doh man, Scripture says he breathed into him the breath of life and Adam became a living soul. The Play-Doh doesn't seem like it's that important in the whole scheme of things. What seems important is whatever God breathed in.

But, when Jesus came, he came in a Play-Doh body. He got hungry and thirsty and tired and knew what it was like to get up in the morning stiff and sore. No other religion even remotely suggests that God ever put himself in a position to feel what you feel. Jesus spent thirty-three years attending to all the problems human beings have in their Play-Doh bodies before he went to the cross to save their souls. Even when he rose from the dead and went back to where he'd come from, Jesus never shed the Play-Doh. He left behind a gaggle of disciples whose souls had been rekindled, and there burned in their eyes a new and wild light. Jesus didn't gather all their little souls together in a basket and take it with him to heaven. Instead, he sent these men and women out in their skins to declare the gospel.

John the Baptist had been the first to declare that the kingdom was near. Later, as he sat in prison, you can't blame him for wondering what kind of kingdom had actually arrived with Jesus. He sent some friends to ask Jesus the question. "Are you the One who is to come, or shall we look for another?" It is interesting that John knew a king was coming with a kingdom in tow. He didn't say, "So, I guess it was all a pipe dream and this is all there is." No, John knew a Savior was coming; he just wanted to know if it was Jesus. Anyway, Jesus responds with, "Go and tell John what you have seen and heard: the blind receive their sight, the lame walk, lepers are cleansed, and the deaf hear, the dead are raised up, the poor have good news preached to them."[56] Jesus said in effect, "Go and tell John that every way Play-Doh can go wrong I am making it right. He will know what that means."

Penguins will walk miles to get to a feeding hole. They saunter across the arctic in their little tuxedos until they find a break in the ice. The fish they need to survive are down there in the water.

On top there's no food at all. Life itself will only be found if they dive into the dark hole in the ice. But there are also leopard seals under the ice. Leopard seals eat penguins like popcorn so they really like to find breaks in the ice too.

So the penguins gather around the hole in their formals and their best manners waiting for someone to dive in. They wait between life and death. The hole represents both, and they hope for someone to lead them to life. Jesus did that for us. He said, "The only way to save your life is to lose it." And then he went to the cross. *Give up, Go to, Be with*. It is the only way to live. "Follow me," Jesus says, as he dives into the hole.

It is the incarnation that makes the Christian understanding of God different from any other. If you are a follower of Christ it is what makes you different, too. I put on my shoes to walk across the muddiness of my backyard and as I do I follow the steps of Jesus. Seventy teenagers laugh and sing their way to a river at midnight and with every step they trace the steps of a King.

It is a Play-Doh world we live in. People living in broken Play-Doh houses with broken Play-Doh marriages. My neighbor lying on a hospital bed with his Play-Doh liver gone bad. But into this world Jesus came, and as he did he entered into all its Play-Dohness. He calls us to do the same. So into the world we go, broken though we are, to participate with Jesus.

The kingdom of God is one where in every way that Play-Doh can go wrong it eventually will be made right. That is why wherever there is suffering in the world you can find followers of this King. So if you are going to follow this one you must find a way to *Give up, Go to, and Be with*. We stand like penguins around the dark hole wondering if it holds life or death. Jesus beckons us to dive in after him and be nourished and thrilled by real life.

BOB

My friend Byron Beebe is an actuary. I'm not exactly sure what an actuary is. But I know it means Byron has a huge brain. A year after Hurricane Katrina hit, Byron answered our church's call to go to New Orleans to help. His crew "mudded out" houses that had been submerged by the floodwaters. Mudding out means you remove all the contents of the house and then strip it down to the bare studs. Many of the homes had not been entered since the evacuation. "It was eerie," he told me, "we'd find pictures on the walls, clothes in the closets, and sheets on the beds."

There was also food in the refrigerators. Byron's eyes grew wide. "Picture your fully stocked refrigerator with no power. Now fill it with filthy water, drain it slowly, and then marinate it in one-hundred-degree heat for a year. The stench was . . . indescribable. We taped and bungeed them shut, but the moment you moved them, they leaked. No dead animal ever smelled that bad. It was rancid, putrid, and loathsome." Some actuaries have a way with words.

I asked Byron if he'd ever consider going back. He smiled. "When do we leave?"

Mitch Gingrich is a lawyer in the prime of his career. He's been my patient for over twenty years and I've been his client for ten. One day Mitch called with some big news. He was uprooting his family and moving halfway around the world to serve international students at the University of Canterbury in Christchurch, New Zealand as a full time missionary. I asked him if it would be tough to walk away from his successful law practice. He grinned and quoted Jim Elliott. "He is no fool who gives what he cannot keep to gain that which he cannot lose."

Another good friend, Vince Petno, is a retired cardiologist. He was also an Academic All-American wide receiver for The Citadel military academy. Vince has dedicated his retirement years to developing ways to use the moringa tree to fight malnutrition in Third World countries. Vince was in Haiti planting, harvesting, planning, teaching and organizing when the big earthquake hit Port Au Prince in January 2010. Getting back home was a major ordeal. A couple weeks later we sat in my kitchen looking at a couple hundred pictures of devastation on his laptop. I asked if the typical cardiologist retirement lifestyle, the one dedicated to comfort and security, looked more appealing after what he'd been through. I'll never forget Vince's response. He stood up and puffed out his chest like he was coming to attention. "Sir. Perfecting my golf swing and collecting seashells just won't do. I can't help myself—I'm driven by gratitude for everything the triune God has done for me. I will stay the course, Sir." I saluted him and we both laughed.

I've been blessed with many great friends like Byron, Mitch, and Vince. Guys who found ways to *give up, go to, and be with* through missions. But now I want to share about two remarkable friends who joined the movement of the incarnation without ever leaving home.

Marshall Brandon is an African-American. He is dark. And he is big. He was born in Huntsville, Alabama in 1948. His father was an illiterate sharecropper and his grandfather had been born into slavery. When Marshall was three years old the family moved to Youngstown, a gritty steel town in Eastern Ohio. Youngstown is a tough place to grow up in the 'hood, but for Marshall the toughest place was not on the street. It was inside the home.

Marshall's mother was a rage-aholic. She'd beat him with an extension cord until he bled. His dad was a fall-down drunk. But Marshall was smart. He eventually honed his street-fighting skills as a way to survive. And as a way to release his inner rage. When he fought his goal was to *really hurt* his enemy. The kids on the street feared him. Marshall was a natural-born leader. By age thirteen he had organized his own gang.

Five years later Marshall decided to get out of the 'hood. Uncle Sam would be his ticket. He enlisted in the Army in 1966 and spent the next year learning a different type of survival—in the jungles of Vietnam. On several occasions he became furious when the Army put black GIs into harm's way while whites sat on the sidelines. Back home, the civil rights movement was in its heyday. And Marshall latched onto every bit of news about it he could get.

171

By the time he left Vietnam, Marshall had the white man in his crosshairs. Marshall wanted vengeance. Vengeance for his grandfather's slavery. Vengeance for the dead black soldiers. Vengeance for all the injustice in America. And he wanted to inflict pain.

Marshall spent the next two years in an ordnance detail at Fort Knox, watching over the arms of the armed forces. Some of what he watched over, he stole. Grenades, guns, ammo, dynamite, an entire arsenal. He planned to join the Black Nationalist Movement in their mission to take Alabama, Louisiana, and Mississippi by force and form a separate black nation. When Marshall received his honorable discharge in 1969, he was an armed revolutionary looking for deployment.

Marshall went back to Ohio to try to enlist his friends in his deadly cause. Instead, they enlisted him in theirs. Heroin. But drugs cost money and Marshall quickly ran out. He had no job so he began to steal to support his habit. He was arrested for armed robbery and spent his twenty-first birthday in the Mansfield Reformatory where *The Shawshank Redemption* was later filmed.

The black inmates quickly recognized Marshall's leadership skills and "elected" him president of the African-American Culture Club, a semi-clandestine organization almost two hundred strong that shared Marshall's hatred of whites. As president of the AACC, Marshall could arrange to meet with the warden whenever he wanted—just like Andy Dufresne in the movie. Why? Because the warden knew this group could mobilize to wage war within the prison at any time. But Marshall's main goal was not to hobnob with the warden. He wanted to get out of prison. There was no use tunneling. This was not Hollywood. So even though he was seething against the white man, on the surface he was a model inmate. After three years he was granted early release for good behavior.

Marshall was free but he had no place to stay. He landed on the doorstep of a halfway house in Akron where he met a white man named Dave Fair. Dave was the most gentle-spirited human being Marshall had ever encountered. And he eventually became the first white man Marshall couldn't hate. Over time, Dave shared the good news with Marshall and a seed was planted.

Six years later the seed finally sprouted and Marshall gave his heart to Christ. He joined an all-black church with his wife, Katika. Before long Marshall was leading a Bible study for black men and volunteering in a prison ministry. He was making good money at Ohio Edison. The couple was blessed with a son and then a daughter. Marshall prayed about going into the ministry. His church ordained him, but no opportunities followed. Several years later, at age forty-six, Marshall was offered his first full-time ministry position. He talked it over with Katika.

"An inner-city homeless shelter?"

"Yeah, baby. It's called The Haven of Rest."

"How much does it pay?"

"Exactly half of what I'm making now."

They laughed until their sides ached. But that night God spoke to Marshall in a dream, "You go. I will give you what you need." The next morning they made the decision. Marshall would *give up* his comfortable income, *go to* homeless men, to *be with* them as a minister of the gospel. Marshall loved his new job and assumed he would be a lifer at The Haven of Rest.

Marshall met Joe Coffey the following year. It was the year 2000 and back then only one black person attended Christ Community Chapel. Joe designed a new position, Pastor for Local Outreach, and offered it to Marshall. The conversation with Katika sounded a little different this time.

"That big church in Hudson?"

"Yeah, baby. Lily-white Hudson."

"Mmm. Let's see. What's wrong with that picture?"

Once again they laughed until their sides ached. A year later Marshall accepted the position. He *gave up* his black comfort zone, to *go to* Hudson, to *be with* white people like me. And in the process he became my first black friend.

Marshall gives me a big hug every time he sees me. Sometimes he even kisses me on the cheek. He's in my inner circle. He's one of the few people I can turn to in times of trouble. If I only had a dollar to my name I would trust Marshall with it. Given all I've told you about him, think about what that means. Marshall and I are friends for life. I think he'd even take a bullet for me.

Sometimes Marshall preaches on Sundays when Joe's on vacation. He looks and sounds totally black. He wants people to shout, "Amen!" But we don't. If someone does, everybody chuckles. In spite of the differences in skin color and cultural background, Marshall feels at home in the predominantly white environment of CCC. He says we are all one big family.

Here's where the story takes another twist. Our church is starting a fourth campus, this one in the inner city of Akron. Guess who's been tapped to be the pastor? So Marshall is preparing to do it all over again. He will *give up* his lily-white church home where he is loved and secure and appreciated, and *go back to* the inner city, to *be with* people that are predominately his own color.

Pastor Marshall Brandon understands the movement of the incarnation. He flows with it. And he is one of the most fully alive and joyful people I've ever met.

When I first met Steve Myers he was a general surgeon with a thriving practice, and a new member of a physician-owned imaging center project I had helped syndicate. One day he was sitting in my home library with a mug of coffee telling me stories about his annual trips to Africa. Steve is developing a hospital for women and children in the Sahara Desert. On one trip he was abducted at gunpoint and held hostage by guerillas. But that's a story for another book.

Steve hadn't come to my home to talk about mission trips. He had big dreams. Literally. He wanted to specialize in bariatric surgery—gastric bypass and LAP-band operations for the treatment of severe obesity. He wanted to *give up* his general surgery practice, *go to* the most disdained subpopulation in American culture, to *be with* them as someone who could help them get their life back. And he wanted my help. I already liked Steve a lot. So I agreed to become his business development consultant.

I was convinced Steve needed a free public seminar so people could meet him in person and hear his message. So I spent an entire day designing Steve's PowerPoint slides. When I was done I patted myself on the back—I knew the presentation was compelling. I also wrote a script to go with it. We met at a nice restaurant for dinner and rehearsed. Steve was pleased.

The night of the seminar came. I arrived early and noticed the extra-wide chairs Steve had rented for the occasion. "Good idea," I told Steve, "I hadn't thought of that." I sat in the back with my legal pad, watching as fifty morbidly obese people slowly, very slowly, filed in and took their seats. Most were accompanied by a spouse, a friend, or a family member. Eventually the lights dimmed and the seminar started. There were thirty slides and my first one simply said, *Welcome!*

Steve began, "I know how you are feeling tonight." That wasn't in the script. "I understand people of size."

People of size? I didn't recognize that either.

"My dad is a brilliant electrical engineer and inventor. But he has struggled with his weight for most of his adult life. I watched it take a toll on his health. I watched people look at him sitting in a restaurant—and then look away in disgust. And even though he was the largest person in the room, he was treated like he was invisible. Or worse. Not a day went by when he was not subjected to ridicule because of his size."

Steve's passion mounted as I wondered when he would get to slide two. "Our society has two categories of people who are considered the least among us. Those in nursing homes, and you. You get little, if any, respect. People think you are lazy. That you don't want to get better. That you have no willpower. But I know there are many pathways and many reasons that lead to your condition. Medical reasons, hereditary reasons, emotional trauma, immobilization from car accidents, side effects of steroids for asthma, just to name a few. And I know that 60 percent of women of size were sexually abused in childhood. People out there think they're better than you. They all have problems too, but they have an advantage. They can usually keep their problems hidden. But you can't fit your obesity in the closet."

This was not what we rehearsed.

"I know you are struggling. I know you feel trapped in an extra-large body. Trapped with your back pain and knee pain and emotional pain and layers of social, psychological, and economic difficulties due to prejudice against people of size. And I know you are dehumanized by their name-calling. But I'm here tonight to tell you there's hope. Our name is Fresh Start Bariatrics. We're here to give you a fresh start.

Steve finally flipped to the second slide, but the word "dehumanized" was stuck in my throat.

How many times had I looked at an obese person, rolled my eyes, and muttered something about a "beached whale," as if they were not even human? I looked around the room and the silent testimony of the friends and family who had come to offer support hit me between the eyes. They knew that these were real people, people with very little hope, people facing severe and seemingly unshakeable problems every day. They understood, and Steve understood. I began to weep. A moment later I was losing it. I headed out the back door because I could not regain my composure. I was so ashamed.

When I came back Steve was rolling through my slides. "Fresh Start ministers to the whole person. We have dieticians, internists, psychologists, mobility specialists—we even have a chaplain. As the surgeon, it's my privilege to be one small part of a team that can help change your life."

Many lives started down a new path that night. Mine included.

After the seminar, a woman approached Steve and told him she couldn't go to the movies with her family because the seats were too small. She thanked him for the oversized chairs he had provided that evening. Susie weighed over three hundred pounds. Four years later, she weighs half that much. She not only goes to the movies, she also enjoys salsa dancing.

For Steve, every day is an adventure. Because every day he *gives up, goes to,* to *be with* people who need a fresh start. To many, he's the hands and feet of Jesus. To me, he's a living reminder of the love, compassion, and mercy that's behind the movement of the incarnation.

15

The Church

Of Blockheads and Magnificence

JOE

I have been part of one church or another my whole life. There are a lot of messed up people in churches. I don't think this is a secret. In fact, organized religion is such an easy target that few secular writers even bother to take shots at the church. It is like shooting fish in a barrel. They leave it to hip Christian writers to point out how irrelevant the modern church has become.

Personally I think the church has always been a mess. Communion Sunday at the church of Corinth in the first century was evidently more like a keg party. Maybe that is why we have to use the tiny little cups now. My guess is that Corinth was still using the big cups. The ancient Thessalonian church was having trouble too. Some yahoos on the membership rolls kept quitting their jobs and running up a hill in white robes and sneakers telling everyone Jesus was coming back. It's not too different today. After the next natural disaster, one prominent Christian or another will make headlines for saying something just plain silly about why so many people died. My point is that if our faith is filled with people who need a Savior, the church will always be filled with people who are half-cracked.

Blame Jesus. Jesus never hung out with a very good crowd. He could have if he wanted to. You realize that don't you? He actually would have fit in better with the people in my neighborhood. They are mostly decent folks. They don't appear to be particularly religious but they are really nice. They don't have big loud parties and I can't remember a single time in the last ten years when the police had to be called for anything except a rabid raccoon under someone's deck. They actually shot the varmint. It was a shocker but that is a whole other story. But Jesus hung out on the other side of the tracks with the druggies and prostitutes. He explained why when he was at a particularly raucous party at the home of a rich man named Levi. A gaggle of really good religious folk asked, "Why them?" and Jesus said, "It is not the healthy who need a doctor. It is the sick. I came to heal the sick ones."[57] And the church has been filled with messed up people ever since.

If I went to an emergency room with a broken finger and saw someone with a gaping wound I wouldn't say, "Hey, you shouldn't be here. You are really messed up." If I had a chance I would probably say something like, "Wow, good thing you got here. You are in rough shape. I hope you make it." That is the church. People sitting around at various stages of being screwed up. Some people come with really big wounds that they'll be dealing with for the rest of their lives. It shouldn't surprise us that church people are easy targets. We didn't get in because we were particularly good. We got in because we particularly needed a savior.

⌒

I was in Florence several years ago and saw the sculpture of David by Michelangelo. In the museum, when you turn this one corner and look down the corridor, suddenly there it is in all of its brilliance, seventeen feet tall. As I walked toward it I noticed other sculptures off to the sides. One in particular is of a man who looks like he is trying to pull himself out of the marble. His torso is partly free and his right arm reaches up to the block of marble that should have been his head. The arm is powerfully flexed but in all the years of flexing he hasn't made a lot of progress. The sculpture appears half finished. Scholars are divided about whether it is actually an unfinished work or precisely what Michelangelo intended. Many believe the great artist was giving us a glimpse of what he could see. Michelangelo claimed he could see what was inside a piece of marble. He felt his job was to free whatever was stuck by knocking off the rock that didn't belong. In this case it was a man.

Anyway, it was very moving to me partly because I feel much more like the guy trying to pull his head out of stone than I feel like David. I want to be like David and of course if I can't be like David the next best thing is for people to *think* I am like David. David stands in a magnificent pose of strength and poise. He is a man who stands with his sling (and that is about his only article of clothing) and is completely relaxed in who he is and what he can do. I, on the other hand, am much more like the poor schlep who is trying to pull his head out of a block of rock.

⌒

I was in India several years ago. Jet lag had me up early and I sat outside an orphanage with my journal and my Bible trying to listen for the voice of God through my rock-hard head. I sat for a long time before the sun began to peek over the horizon. I had already written several pages. I praised and I thanked and I repented and I tried to love this invisible God who seemed to be more elusive than most religious people will admit. Finally I put my pen down and just sat in silence.

It was a single sentence. I am not sure if it was God or just a sudden burst of truth that finally made its way in. Maybe there is not much difference. This is the truth that came to me that early morning on the other side of the world. "You are trying too hard to love me—it is much more important for you to experience my love for you than it is for me to experience your love for me." That was it.

There is a scene in the movie *As Good As It Gets*. Jack Nicholson is trying to express his feelings to Helen Hunt. He stumbles around and finally says, "You make me want to be a better man." Outside that orphanage I finally had a reason to become a better man. The God of the universe looked at me with my head still stuck in so much marble and essentially said, "I love you even though you aren't anything like David. It is my love that will be the hammer and chisel."

In the Gospel of Mark the very first words Jesus speaks are, "The time is fulfilled, and the kingdom of God is at hand; repent and believe in the gospel."[58] The gospel is this good news: God demonstrates his love toward me in that while I am still a sinner Christ died for me.[59] Repent means to turn away from something you have been doing or believing, and do or believe something else. My biggest problem is I keep thinking God could only love someone like David so I keep trying to pull my own head out of the marble so he will love me. "Repent!!!" Jesus says, "And believe the good news. You are already loved so let the love of God set you free."

I was walking toward the magnificent statue of David. The corridor was flanked on both sides by unfinished pieces of rock. Men writhing to climb out of the stone that held them fast. By the time I stood to admire the wonder and beauty of David, my appreciation for Michelangelo was very great indeed. It was the unfinished man that gave me appreciation for what Michelangelo was able to do. That is the way the church is supposed to work. The church is filled with people only Jesus could love and he wouldn't want it any other way.

It is our cracks that might be the most important thing about us. It is cracks that let grace in. It is cracks that eventually show forth glory. Grace in and glory out. David would be easy to love. What's not to love about perfection? But loving someone like me is a different story. It is only when you know how terribly selfish and unlovable I am that you can begin to grasp the depth of the love of my Savior.

Before Saul became Paul he hated the church. He went from town to town dragging Christians out for beatings or prison or both. On the road to Damascus he had an encounter with the living Lord. Jesus appeared and blinded him with brilliance. Saul heard only a voice. The voice said, "Saul, Saul, why do you persecute me?" Saul must have sat there confused. It was never his intent to pick on someone so scary and so bright. Jesus indentified himself so closely with the church that to persecute the church was to persecute him. Jesus would call Saul out like a piece of throwaway marble. He was transformed by the love of the One who called him. Paul was blind and then he could see, and the thing he saw when he looked at the church was something Jesus loved dearly.

There is no one who loves the church more than Jesus. I remind myself of that every time I look out into a congregation filled with knuckleheads. And I remind myself that the biggest knucklehead of all is about to preach.

BOB

You wouldn't know it from the very English surname, "Bevington," but if it weren't for my dad's dad, I would be a full-blooded Italian. My dad's mother was born in Naples, came over young, and became thoroughly Americanized. But both of my mom's parents were serious Old-World Italians and stayed that way till their dying breath. Their real names were Pasquale and Assunta but they went by Patsy and Sue. Being Italian was a bright spot in my childhood. My grandpa played an old concertina, a small, simplified accordion. My eight cousins and I would gather around and glow whenever he played it. All my cousins were full-blooded Italians. But they overlooked my impure pedigree and called me their *paisano*. That always made me happy.

I took my mom to Italy a couple years after my dad died. It was just the two of us. We toured Tuscany as spring gave way to summer and the sun drenched the landscape. Thanks to mom's wheelchair the entire trip moved in slow motion. We lingered over the beauty of the scenery, the people, and the food. No one spoke our language, yet we felt totally at home and connected. That's probably why I had so many epiphanies there.

The first one happened in Firenze. Joe called it Florence, but we call it Firenze because we're Italian. I, too, stood in front of the magnificent statue of David. But it was his right hand that caught my attention. It is huge. And it is perfect. I tried to place my own hand into the exact same position. That's when I discovered the magic. My hand can move. David's might be perfect, but mine is alive. I've been watching the movement and marveling at it ever since.

Early the next morning I wheeled Mom out and stood next to her on the paving stones outside the three-hundred-year-old villa where we were staying. Mist hung over terraced vineyards as far as our eyes could see. That's when I truly noticed it for the first time. Air. If you stop and think about it, air is miraculous. It's invisible stuff that you breathe in for a few seconds, and then you breathe it back out, and somehow it does something in you that keeps you alive. In an act of celebration I closed my eyes and sucked in air until my lungs were bursting with delight. Then I squeezed it all out and repeated the cycle several times. When I finally opened my eyes my mom was doing the same thing. Italian air is amazing. But so is the air you're breathing right now.

The third epiphany was the best one. It was after midnight. Mom had gone to bed but I was wide-awake so I went outside. The air was the perfect temperature where you can't even feel it. I looked up and saw the most glorious sky I have ever seen. Clearer than it was in Alaska. God's fingernail of a moon kept watch over millions of stars. The 60s song "Everybody Is a Star" came to mind. It's a cool song and the title speaks volumes. It's saying that every person who lives and breathes radiates something glorious like starlight. I closed my eyes as warm thoughts of the people we met in the nearby village filled my mind. They were stars. I smiled as I envisioned the ones who tried to speak English using only pure Italiano plus passionate hand gestures. Glorious stars. I thought about all the people living all over the world at that very moment, breathing and moving their hands.

When I opened my eyes a really bright star got my attention. I honed in on it and discovered it was actually two stars that had come into alignment. That's why it was so bright. It occurred to me that people can do that, too. Maybe you and I will meet someday and the star that is you and the star that is me will line up. If we do, the glory we give off can be beyond addition. Like one plus one equals three.

But the epiphany didn't end there. I suddenly remembered a line from the song that posed the question, "Ever catch a fallen star?" That is probably *the* question when it comes to relationships. In this world, everybody is a star, but a fallen one. We are all self-eclipsed by our own sin. So bringing our fallen stars into alignment is tricky business. I think that's why people continually look for something to align themselves *with*. Something outside themselves. Something to have in common. It might be a hobby. A political cause. An irritating co-worker. It can be anything. Even a beverage. If we find alignment with just the right something, another star might join us and together we might be able to bask in a little glory for a while.

⌒

Large groups of people sometimes attempt to align themselves with something big. When this works it can be quite exhilarating. Like on January 3, 2003, when Ohio State played Miami in the Fiesta Bowl for the National Championship. Buckeye fans started swarming nine hours before the kick-off. As I walked down the street it was as if I had seventy thousand best friends—all because I was wearing scarlet and gray clothes, a Woody hat, and several necklaces made of buckeyes. Total strangers of all ages were high-fiving me. Some offered me brats and beers. I exchanged email addresses with several of them as if we'd be friends forever and do business deals and go on fishing trips together. But in reality those new relationships were false alignments. The stars in the Pleiades look close, but they are actually light-years apart.

Of course, Ohio State won the game in double overtime as time stood still for the Buckeye Nation. But on my way back to the car a guy with a scarlet and gray face puked on my shoes. That took a little of the shine off for me. The Arizona desert air didn't smell quite as fragrant after that. There are glory-muting blockheads in every crowd.

I think it's safe to say that genuine and lasting alignments between individuals are rare. And the odds get worse the more people you add to the mix. Christians are no exception. Joe did a good job of pointing that out. But there's another side to the story.

<hr />

When Jesus is the "big thing" people attempt to align themselves with, real glory can happen. Like sitting around a campfire discussing the gospel with close friends at Walden Pond until the wee hours. Or in an upper room on a missionary campus in India singing praise songs with our team. Or in a circle of prayer after Bible study on a Sunday night. And especially in our regular Sunday morning worship services at Christ Community Chapel. Somehow alignment happens in spite of the presence of a blockhead like me. And in the process, many—maybe not all—but many, are drenched in glory. How can that be?

The first clue is that the fallen stars are not the only stars present. Jesus is there, too. In the very last chapter of the Bible, Jesus says, "I am the root and the descendant of David, the bright morning star."[60] Fully God and fully man, Jesus is the only human star that has not fallen, and he promised, "Where two or three are gathered in my name, there am I among them."[61] His presence makes the most ordinary place brilliant and special beyond imagination. Nothing in Firenze or Rome or the universe can compare.

Another clue is that all or some of the people in those alignments *love* Jesus. Peter summed it up in a single verse that is among my favorites. It's 1 Peter 1:8, which says, "Though you have not seen him, you love him. Though you do not now see him, you believe in him and rejoice with joy that is inexpressible and filled with glory." So when people who love Jesus get together and rejoice like this, since each of them is already filled, the glory simply spills over onto those around them. You've probably seen this. It happens regularly in lots of churches. If you come to our church and worship with Rob Thomas or Marshall Brandon or Tom Randall you'll see what I mean.

A third clue comes from a verse that might contain the seven most mysterious words in the entire Bible. "Christ in you, the hope of glory."[62] Christ is the most glorious being in the Universe. His glory is immeasurable. So if the infinitely glorious Christ is *in* a person, what can that mean? And what can it mean when two or more persons with Christ in them come into alignment?

Every true believer in Christ has experienced brokenness over his or her sin. So when they see sin in another person, it looks familiar—it looks like their own. That's when empathy and deep understanding become possible.

Every true believer has experienced the grace of being forgiven on behalf of Christ's sacrifice. So when they are offended by another, they know where to take it—to the cross. To the unique place where genuine forgiveness and lasting reconciliation can be found. And when this happens, it's glorious. Like Rita and Amy worshiping side-by-side in our church on a Sunday morning.

Your local church might very well be the best place for you on the planet. If it's a place where Jesus is. If it's a place where some of the people love Jesus, and have Jesus in them. If it's a place where broken people with authentic faith experience confrontations with grace. A place like that can become irresistible to any fallen star.

The wonderful thing about Jesus Christ is that there are so many things about him you can be sure of. One of these is that he loves the church. He loves the church so much he gave himself up for her. That's Ephesians 5:25. There's significance in the fact that the Bible refers to the church as *her*. Try to fathom the meaning of the astonishing words Paul writes a few verses later: "'Therefore a man shall leave his father and mother and hold fast to his wife, and the two shall become one flesh.' This mystery is profound, and *I am saying that it refers to Christ and the church*."

That can only mean one thing: Christ loves the church so much he intends to *marry* her! He desires to hold her close and, in some spiritual way that applies only to God, become one with her. That is an unimaginable level of alignment. But it will happen. And it will be glorious. John saw an astonishing vision announcing it. He later gave this report:

> Then I heard what seemed to be the voice of a great multitude, like the roar of many waters and like the sound of mighty peals of thunder, crying out, "Hallelujah! For the Lord our God the Almighty reigns. Let us rejoice and exult and give him the glory, for the marriage of the Lamb has come, and his Bride has made herself ready. . . ."[63]

Then an angel told John to write something encouraging: "Blessed are those who are invited to the marriage supper of the Lamb." John smiled. But the angel wanted to make sure John knew the source, "These are the true words of God."

Jesus loves the church so much, it is inevitable—he *will* have her as his Bride. His excitement for her cannot be contained. And he wants us to know it. He wants us all, together as one body, to long for him as much as he longs for us. Christ loves the church with passion and resolve. He is able, and he is eager, to transform us into something irresistibly beautiful. As unbelievable as this may sound, the church will be his crowning glory and bring him great pleasure, far more than anything else he has made. And, knowing where this is all headed, he loves the church with a perfect and infinite love right now, at this very moment.

I hope you take a few moments to let that sink in before we go on.

How much does Jesus love the church? Enough to pay an unimaginable price to bring her into complete alignment with himself. His hands tell the story. They are wonderful hands. Hands that fashioned the Universe. "All things were created through him and for him."[64] Hands that took on flesh and became tiny baby hands. Hands that became tough as he practiced a carpenter's trade. Hands that healed lepers and gave sight to the blind. Hands that popped open the ears of the deaf and blessed little children. Perfect hands whose movements were always innocent and sinless. Hands that were nailed to a cross with nine-inch iron spikes. Bloody hands that ceased moving so that ours could move forever. That's how much he loves the church. His hands bear scars at this very moment as he sits at the right hand of the Majesty on High, pleading our case and praying for us and waiting eagerly for the big day. The day he takes our hand in his and makes us his Bride forever.

There's another thing that tells the story of his love. Air. In the beginning, through Jesus, God spoke air into existence. Then he formed man out of the dust and breathed into his nostrils the breath of life. But Jesus did not count his equality with God a thing to be grasped; he emptied himself and took on flesh and lungs and the need for air to stay alive.[65] Then he breathed out so many wonderful words. Words that thousands of years later still bring hope and meaning. One day he arched his back and breathed his last, screaming at the top of his lungs, "It is finished."[66] He suffocated to death so that we could live and breathe forever. That's how much he loves his Bride. When the awestruck centurion saw the way Jesus took his last breath he whispered, "Truly this man was the Son of God!" He was right. On the morning of the third day Jesus came out of the tomb, breathing. And later that night he breathed on his fallen-star, blockhead disciples and they received the Holy Spirit.[67] The world has never been the same, because at that moment the church was born.

So when you walk out of your church feeling indignant, and justified at being disappointed or critical, remember—you, too, are a fallen star and a blockhead, just like every other person in that place. When you feel like keeping Jesus but quitting the church, remember who she is—the precious Bride of Christ. Can you really love him without loving her? Isn't being a member of her this world's highest privilege? Don't miss out on the privilege just because she's still imperfect.

Jesus won't have it any other way. I *must* love the church. I must "1 Corinthians thirteen" her, the chapter that says "Love is patient and kind . . . love does not insist on its own way . . . love is not irritable or resentful . . . Love bears all things, believes all things, hopes all things, endures all things."

God, help me keep this fallen star in alignment with her. Because Jesus loves her.

16

Longing for Paradise

JOE

I am usually not good at solitude. I don't know many people who are. Problem is we are too used to noise. We have radios and TVs, laptops and cellphones and iWhatevers. Every once in a while I need to get away and find quiet. I have learned that quiet is something you must search for and when you finally chase it down it can be almost deafening.

Not too long ago I went outside to look for quiet. I found her by a stone wall. I just sat on the wall breathing and looking around and eventually I began to feel it. The ache. It is not exactly sadness but there is sadness in it. It is a longing. I think noise keeps most people from feeling it. It is because of the ache that we can't even go for a walk without ear buds blasting distraction into our brains.

I sat on the wall in the quiet and let my soul settle into the ache. I happened to look down at some ants. They were working on carving up a Saltine and carrying the pieces off to their ant city somewhere down the stone wall. Each ant would hoist a chunk of cracker in his jaws and heroically begin to carry it who knows how far. They never hesitated. As far as I could tell no ant was slacking by hiding out over against the wall smoking a little ant cigarette. There wasn't a big ant with a particularly large hunk of cracker slipping off to some hideaway so he could provide himself with cracker insurance for a rainy day. There was no squabbling or fighting. Not even when one ant took a short cut across another one's back. They just worked together to make sure everyone was provided for. Every once in a while they would meet each other on the path and rub antennae and give each other a couple of attaboys, and then they would scurry on to see if anyone needed help. I watched for a while and decided that ants don't sin. I also realized that the whole time I was watching I didn't ache.

G. K. Chesterton once said that human beings are the only wild animal. All other animals pretty much act like they were created to act. But humans are in rebellion so we are always acting against our created design.

I was thinking of how the ants would have behaved if they all had rebellious human natures. The whole scene would have been a mess. The first ant to discover the cracker mother lode would have tried to haul it off all by himself. He probably would have pulled a muscle (do ants have hamstrings?) or given himself a hernia (I don't even want to know). Other ants would have heard him scream and come running. It would have been crazy from that point on. There would have been fights, little ant gangs showing up with tiny bandanas, really hungry ants eating as much as they could hold while the others fought. It would be a total fiasco. Years later I would look down and every ant would have an iPod and music would be blaring. Every little anthill would have that eerie blue light coming out of the window from the flat screen on the wall. All the noise would keep them away from the ache.

My world feels broken and it makes me sad. If G. K. Chesterton is right then it is not just my world that is broken, it is me. Human beings are broken. We are not what we could be, should be, want to be. That is the ache I feel when I let silence drown out the noise. I have a longing for paradise.

In the very beginning there was paradise. Adam was placed in a garden and he had everything. Not only did Adam have everything he could possibly want, he also had the unique ability to appreciate beauty. God created all that exists and he made one creature who could appreciate it. My dog never sits and watches the sunset and sighs. The most human thing my dog does is look slightly embarrassed while doing her business on the lawn. She hunches and looks over her shoulder at me and I dutifully look away and let her have some dog privacy. Other than that she is all dog, which means she does not understand the wonder of Mozart or why real jazz lovers can't stand Kenny G.

God created man with the unique capacity to appreciate all the rest of creation. The ability to appreciate it is one of God's great gifts to us. God made beauty for us. Have you ever been able to watch a thunderstorm roll on a summer evening and smell the air change as the drops begin to fall? Have you walked on a beach and looked out at water ten different shades of green and blue while the waves crash and the water sweeps up to your feet? Every single thing you find beautiful or wondrous is a gift for you. God didn't have to give you the ability to appreciate any of it. There is no other animal on the planet with that gift.

God breathed into Adam the breath of life and with that breath came the gift. On the very first morning, God woke Adam up and said, "Hey, get up. I want you to see this. I made this for you to enjoy. Look!" And God pointed to the sun rising in the east exploding in colors and setting the sky itself on fire.

It was not the sunrise that made it paradise. It was the harmony. We still have sunrises, but sunrise does not really take the ache away. It might mask it for a while but the ache is still in the background because it is the harmony that is missing. The ability to appreciate and experience beauty is a reminder that harmony is possible. Beauty calls to my soul and to yours. It says—Look, harmony! We ache because the harmony is so lovely yet so incomplete, so fragile and rare and elusive.

Beauty reminds us we were made for harmony, for paradise. Adam sits with God looking at the sunrise and everything in his world is in a state of unbroken relationship. All of it. He sits with God without guilt and without shame. The presence of God is nothing but sheer pleasure for Adam. He doesn't hide, he doesn't grovel for forgiveness, his mind doesn't race, wondering if he has some unconfessed sin lurking in the shadows. He is in a perfect relationship with his God and with his world. He is not filling the garden with used plastic water bottles or digging huge holes looking for gold. His treasure is right beside him. He sits watching a sunrise with the One who created him and he is at peace at every level and in every way. The Hebrews called it shalom. Shalom is the wholeness of life. It is harmony with God, with people, with creation itself. It is what you were made for. The lack of it causes your soul to ache. And beauty is the reminder of what you long for and what you have lost.

The longing we have for harmony and wholeness is so strong that the lack of it causes people to doubt the existence of God. I hear it all the time. How can there be a God with all the suffering and poverty, all the disease and violence that fills the world? Everyone knows deep down this is not the way things should be. The fabric of the world is so torn, how will it ever be made whole again?

The Gospel accounts of Jesus reveal someone on a mission. It is obvious that Jesus came to die on the cross. The first step toward shalom would be to heal our relationship with God and that would require the cross. But the Gospels also show Jesus constantly moved by compassion. The sick would come to him and, moved with compassion, he would make them whole. Jesus came to make people whole.

Jesus came declaring the coming of a kingdom. This kingdom is characterized by wholeness. It starts with the individual recovery of relationship with God but it doesn't stop there. Jesus described the kingdom with these words, "the blind receive their sight and the lame walk, lepers are cleansed and the deaf hear, and the dead are raised up, and the poor have good news preached to them."[68]

Jesus came to create a community of followers who are being healed of their own brokenness. He expects that community to move out into the world and begin to sew up the torn fabric that's all around us. A follower of Jesus who is not working to re-establish shalom on the earth is not really following.

This is why everywhere the fabric of the world is torn you will find Christians. We feed the hungry, visit the prisoners, heal the lepers, love the outcasts, and bring good news to the poor. We sit with the grieving, hold those who weep, listen to the ones who have no voice, fight for the powerless. We do what our Savior did when he walked the earth. Christianity was never intended to be a non-stop country club experience. You are called to heal the world. Do not miss it.

There is a longing inside every human soul for shalom. Instead of harmony there is brokenness. There are people you rub shoulders with every day who are living in torn-up worlds. The writer to the Hebrews calls Christians a holy nation. The word he uses is *ethnos*. It is the equivalent of the English word, *ethnic*. We use the word ethnic to describe a particular group of people who are connected in some deep, essential way. Jesus intended to create a whole new people group. We are bound together by the common bond of belonging to a different kingdom. We have been brought back into relationship with the true King. The deepest part of us has been healed and now we move out into the world as a force of healing.

This is a book about brokenness and grace and redemption. There are a thousand ways to be broken and only one way to be made whole. There are two amazing things about Christianity. The first is the power and magnificence of grace and what it does as it sinks deeper and deeper into a soul. The second is the plan of God to allow us to participate in his plan to heal the world. Don't miss either one. Your life was never intended to be muted and dulled by weak pleasures. Your life was intended to burn with a dazzling light. You are made to be a part of a new people. You are made for nothing less than to partner with the God of the universe in sewing back together the pieces of the torn-up world we have. The torn part of the fabric is very close to you. Don't miss it.

BOB

Amy and I were headed for Israel and I was pumped. I couldn't wait to stand at the spot where Jesus died on the cross. I planned to experience extraordinary closeness with him there and then fill my pockets with dirt from that place. But I'd have to wait because Golgotha was one of the last stops on our itinerary. We left Grace and Michael in the capable hands of my former wife, Rita.

Our entourage included Joe and Karen and eighteen other couples. After we arrived in Tel Aviv, a motorcoach took us to a hotel in Tiberius where our balcony overlooked the Sea of Galilee. We visited all kinds of cool places in that region. The Mount of Loaves and Fishes where Jesus fed the five thousand. Cana where he turned the water into wine. Capernaum where we saw the remains of Peter's house. Knowing that Jesus spent many nights there gave all of us a warm, fuzzy feeling.

Early one misty morning we took a boat ride on the Sea of Galilee. It was surreal. We could almost see Jesus walking on the water. We could almost hear him calm the raging storm. "Peace! Be still!"[69] We gazed at the shore where the resurrected Christ called out to his weary disciples who fished all night and caught nothing,[70] "Let your net down on the right side of the boat." They ate fish for breakfast that morning, and after our boat ride we'd eat some of the descendants of those fish for lunch.

My anticipation heightened the night we arrived in Jerusalem and checked into the Crowne Plaza Hotel. We got up early the next morning and headed to the Mount of Olives. We walked down Palm Sunday Road[71] and I envisioned the crowd of people spreading their cloaks before him shouting, "Blessed is the King who comes in the name of the Lord!" Some of the Pharisees said to him, "Teacher, rebuke your disciples." Jesus answered, "I tell you the truth, if these were silent, the very stones would cry out." I bent over and picked up a stone and slipped it into my pocket.

In the garden of Gethsemane there are nine olive trees that are more than 2,500 years old. They stand in an area protected by a black, wrought iron fence. We gazed at them in wonder, knowing that if these trees could talk they'd tell us the story of that one awful night, unfolding it scene by scene. Jesus sweating great drops of blood. An angry mob arriving with swords and clubs. He is betrayed with a kiss. Peter cuts off the ear of the high priest's servant; Jesus puts it back on. All his friends desert him, and a young man runs away, naked. I stuck my hand inside the fence and touched one of the trees and felt connected to it all.

Over the next few days we found ourselves in, around, and under Jerusalem. The Pool of Bethesda, the Upper Room, the Shepherd's Field, and more. One day we donned loaner yamakas and approached the Western Wall. There was some passionate prayer going on there. They don't call it the Wailing Wall for no reason. Jews consider themselves to be in the Divine Presence there because they believe the temple is the home of God on earth. And this wall is pretty much all that remains of the temple. I couldn't tell if anyone was experiencing any shalom at the Wall, but it didn't look like it to me.

⌒

The day I'd been waiting for finally arrived. We started at the Church of Ecce Homo. Its name is Latin for Pontius Pilate's famous statement, "Behold the man."[72] The church is built over The Stone Pavement—the place where Pilate pronounced the death sentence on Jesus. We walked down a series of staircases and there it was. I stepped on the stone and a chill went down my spine knowing that Jesus stood right there two thousand years ago with his back ripped open, wearing a crown of thorns. A few yards away we could see the beginning of the Via Dolorosa—the Way of the Blood of his Suffering. It marks the route Jesus and the cross took on the way to Golgotha. I whispered to Joe, "We're getting close."

All of this was underground like pretty much all of Old Jerusalem. Not a lot of it has been excavated. So to follow the Via Dolorosa from there you have to climb back up the stairs and go out onto the cobblestone street and follow the signs. I was not prepared for what happened next.

The street was narrow and so crowded with people there was no room for cars. It was lined with shops and snack bars. Vendors hawked everything from cheesy olivewood trinkets, to backgammon boards, to pots and pans, to water pipes that looked like bongs for a party of five. "I make you good deal, three for price of one." I don't know if they were Jews or Palestinians or opportunistic Christians or what. But they were making a carnival out of my Savior's death march. Several of them said, "We love you, even if you not buy from us." My head began spinning. Amy held my hand so tight I knew she was on the verge of crying. I looked straight ahead, trying in vain to ignore everything I saw and heard. "We love America. We love Obama. Come back, we make you good deal." I whispered to Karen Coffey, "This is messed up."

We arrived at the end of the Via Dolorosa. The place I'd been longing for. Golgotha—the Place of the Skull. Only to discover it's inside a church, the Church of the Holy Sepulchre. My heart was pounding as we went inside. It was very ornate, very dark, and very crowded. We were told that to see the place where the cross once stood you had to climb up a marble staircase that was jammed with tourists. Not all of our entourage was up for it. But Joe, Karen, Amy, and I were determined to see it and so were a dozen others from our group. When we finally got to the ultra-gilded room at the top we discovered a piece of plate glass in the floor. Under it was a piece of bedrock. Golgotha. A few feet away there was an elaborate altar. Under the altar was a tile mosaic surrounding a six-inch round hole. People were crammed together waiting their turn to crawl under the altar one at a time and place their hand into the hole that once held the cross. We never got to the hole. We didn't even get close. A security guard shooed Joe and I away a couple times when we tried to get close enough to take a picture.

We eventually gave up and headed back down the steps. When we reached the main floor we could see the site of the Holy Sepulchre—the tomb where the body of Jesus was laid until he rose again on the third day. It was inside an aedicule—a shrine—that seemed to be surrounded by ornate curtains like the ones in *The Wizard of Oz*. I couldn't tell if people were getting behind the curtains, but at that point I didn't even care. I was disturbed at the core of my being and I just wanted to get out of there. I walked out into the bright sunshine and looked at my companions. I was searching for some words of wisdom and comfort. But everybody, even Joe, looked dumbfounded. I left the scene with empty pockets.

On the ride back to the hotel I thought about the cross. I decided I was glad it's not still around. People would probably worship it. Some might wage war over it. Others might try to sell it for a big profit on eBay. Especially if it came with a certificate of authenticity.

Back at the hotel the last thing Amy and I wanted to do was socialize over another buffet dinner. So we spent five minutes eating and headed up to our room. I flopped my weary body onto the bed and did something I rarely do. I grabbed the remote and turned on the TV. I couldn't get it to work, so Amy took over and eventually found a movie in English. *Wall Street*, with Michael Douglas and Charlie Sheen. It's a movie about greed and corruption and disappointment, but it all seemed acceptable since it was happening in New York and not the Holy Land. It comforted me by drowning out the memory of the voices I heard on the Via Dolorosa. Amy fell asleep within ten minutes. My eyelids were heavy but I forced myself to stay awake until the credits rolled.

I turned off the TV and the room went dark. I was physically exhausted and emotionally drained. But in the quiet of that hotel room I ached so badly I couldn't sleep. So I prayed. Something I hadn't done much of all day.

How could you allow this mess to happen?

After a prolonged moment of silence I decided to get specific about my angst. *Why does the Dome of the Rock sit on top of the Holy of Holies? What's up with the hole and the Wizard of Oz curtains and the buzzards along the Via Dolorosa? Why?*

The prayer became more like a nightmare. I could feel my heart pounding. And then out of nowhere I could almost hear his voice:

Bob. Where am I?

What do you mean, Lord?

Why do you look for the living among the dead?

A Bible verse rocketed into my head, *"After making purification for sins, he sat down at the right hand of the Majesty on high."*[73]

I took a deep breath and slowly let all the air out. I looked at Amy. She was fast asleep. I smiled and said out loud, "He is not here, for he has risen."

The image of a bird hatching came into my mind. The bird flies away, never to return to visit its empty eggshell. It doesn't grow up and bring its little birdie babies back to get all melancholy over the remains. The eggshell is not what's beautiful, the living bird is. Jesus rose from the dead, leaving the bedrock of Golgotha and the empty tomb behind. His glory is not the least bit diminished by the condition of the relics.

Suddenly I felt total relief—but it gets even better. He continued to whisper in the darkness.

"Nevertheless, I tell you the truth: it is to your advantage that I go away, for if I do not go away, the Helper will not come to you. But if I go, I will send him to you."[74]

We were having a much-needed, sacred conversation. I responded.

Wow. You left this place behind and sent your Spirit to indwell us. We carry the temple within us wherever we go. We don't need a holy mountain or city or shrine. Not even a special wall. We can worship in spirit and in truth anywhere on the planet.

A renewed appreciation for his brilliance came over me. But he wasn't done with me yet.

The Palm Sunday Road. You were there.

That's when it hit me. The last time Jesus was there he looked out over Jerusalem and wept. I flipped on a light, opened my Bible, and found the words he spoke through his tears:

Would that you, even you, had known on this day the things that make for peace! But now they are hidden from your eyes. For the days will come upon you, when your enemies will set up a barricade around you and surround you and hem you in on every side and tear you down to the ground, you and your children within you. And they will not leave one stone upon another in you, because you did not know the time of your visitation.[75]

Jesus had indeed prophesied this mess. None of it caught him by surprise. With that reassurance I thanked him for his sovereignty, closed my eyes, and fell asleep.

⸻

I awoke at the crack of dawn, grabbed my Bible, and headed for the balcony. From the fifteenth floor the city of Jerusalem was a silhouette against the early morning glow. It reminded me of the New Jerusalem in the book of Revelation, so I quickly turned to that page. What I read there took my breath away:

And I saw the holy city, new Jerusalem, coming down out of heaven from God, prepared as a bride adorned for her husband. And I heard a loud voice from the throne saying, "Behold, the dwelling place of God is with man. He will dwell with them, and they will be his people, and God himself will be with them as their God. He will wipe away every tear from their eyes, and death shall be no more, neither shall there be mourning, nor crying, nor pain anymore, for the former things have passed away." And he who was seated on the throne said, "Behold, I am making all things new."[76]

Shalom will arrive right on schedule. His Bride's brokenness — all of it — will be made whole forever. Our longings will be fulfilled in unbroken, harmonious relationship with him. His presence will be paradise forever. My heart filled with gratitude and I thanked him repeatedly.

Just then my entire life kind of flashed before my eyes. I say kind of because it was soft, not scary. Even though it included my dad and Ricky and porn addiction and adultery and lying and pride and a hundred sins I'd committed just since we arrived in the Holy Land. I calmly acknowledged that the only reason I wasn't freaking out about my past was because of Jesus and all he did here. But then I wondered about where life would take me — how I would get from where I stood on the balcony to my place in the New Jerusalem. That's when the conversation resumed.

Trust Me.

I thought about the nation of Israel. And of all the enemies that tried to enslave or eradicate it over thousands of years. I can't even name them all. But there were Canaanites, Amorites, Hittites, Assyrians, Babylonians, Persians, Romans, Ottomans, Nazis, and Palestinians. A remnant always remained. I looked out on the land promised to Abraham and saw a blue and white flag bearing the Star of David waving in the breeze.

"I trust you, Lord."

I turned around and thought to myself, *It doesn't get any better than this.* I was wrong, as he was about to show me.

Amy got up and sensed my personal shalom. She listened intently as I filled her in. Then she hugged me and I felt healing move from my soul to hers. As she clung to me I wondered how the rest of our group was doing. When we arrived at breakfast I discovered most of them looked happy and refreshed. I imagined all the sacred conversations that must have gone on simultaneously during the night. And I pretty much kept my story to myself. Until now.

Later that day we had communion together in a tranquil garden. We sang and worshiped and partook of broken bread and the cup of the New Covenant in his blood. I became aware of something amazing. A *community* wholeness. A *corporate* shalom. A little preview of the New Jerusalem unfolded right before my eyes. Nothing in this world could be better than that.

17

Why Grace Always Flows Red

JOE

The garden of Gethsemane has always been a little troubling to me. Jesus is a mess. It is the night before the crucifixion. For ten chapters he has been talking about his death. He has even told his disciples how he was going to die. On the way to Jerusalem he said, "The Son of Man will be delivered over to the chief priests and scribes, and they will condemn him to death and deliver him over to the Gentiles to be mocked and flogged and crucified, and he will be raised on the third day."[77] The mode of death should not have been any great surprise. And yet in the garden we find him begging to get out of it. He is so distraught the gospel writer says he is sweating great drops of blood. He is really a mess. It couldn't have been the physical death as tortuous as it was. In the years to come countless disciples would face crucifixion as martyrs and do it while singing hymns. If it was the physical suffering he was dreading then he just was not very brave. But of course that doesn't fit the character of Jesus as we find him in Scripture. The thing that was making him come undone was what he simply referred to as "the cup." "Father, if it be possible, let this cup pass from me." The question then becomes, what was the cup? Or maybe more importantly, what was in the cup?

I saw a game show a couple of years ago. It was short-lived because it was excruciating to watch. It was called *The Moment of Truth*. The contestants were hooked up to a lie detector and then asked a series of questions. If they could answer twenty-one questions without lying then they would win $500,000. The questions were designed to expose the part of them they least wanted anyone to know. If the lie detector buzzed then they lost all the money. I watched one woman make it to the $100,000 mark. She had answered truthfully that she had lied to an employer, stolen from an employer, would rather give food to a dog than to a homeless person, was sorry she married her present husband, and wished she had married an old boyfriend. The question that moved her to $100,000 was if she had ever had sex with another man while married to her present husband. She answered, "Yes" and the crowd erupted. Both the husband and the mother of the woman put their heads in their hands and began to cry.

The next question seemed like the easiest question she had been asked all night. "Are you a good person?" That was it. I breathed a sigh of relief because I thought this question would at least not shatter another life. Everyone watching had been a witness to this woman filling a cup with the sludge of her life. She thought for a minute and then answered, "Yes, I am a good person." The buzzer went off. She had lied. After all those questions, all that sludge, all that pain, the buzzer sounded and she lost everything. She desperately wanted to believe she was a good person. We all do. But the questions asked had brought up so much sludge that even she was convinced in the deeper recesses of her soul that she was not good.

I sat on my couch and wondered how many questions God would have to ask me before my cup was filled with sludge and I would hang my head and admit I am not good. I don't think it would take very long for me. I don't know you but my guess is it wouldn't take very long for you either. So, there we sit with

God. Our heads hanging, our hearts broken, and a cup full of sludge at our feet. Now what?

Jesus knelt in the garden and asked a question. He asked if there was any way other than drinking the cup. He was asking a popular question. Jesus was asking if there is some other way a human being could become reconciled to God. As a pastor I get asked that a lot. People will say, "Christianity is so exclusive. What about all the other religions? What about really good people?" Those are basically the same questions Jesus asked in the garden. He knelt while sweating great drops of blood and asked, "What about other religions? What if someone is very sincere? Can't someone be a really good person and make it?" The problem has always been the cup. No other religion deals with the cup. It's the cup we have filled just by being us.

God does not pardon. American presidents have a constitutional power to pardon, and when they are about to leave office they like to use it because they pretty much have nothing to lose. They choose some people who have been convicted of crimes and no matter what they did their sentences are commuted and they go free. There are always some people who get really upset about this, including the victims of those crimes. I think I understand. When a president pardons someone, it is an act of grace but not justice. For justice to be served a price must be paid. That is why God does not pardon.

People ask, "If God wants to forgive someone then why doesn't he just forgive them? Why the whole cross thing?" This is why. In a pardon the cup is ignored, but for true forgiveness to happen grace and justice have to meet. Someone must drink the cup or there's no justice. No actual righting of a wrong. Now, whoever drinks the cup is going to scream, "My God, my God, why have you forsaken me?" If a human being drinks his own cup he will scream. When Jesus drank the cup for us, he screamed. The reason

207

is the cup burns like hell going down. That is the truth. Grace always flows red like blood.

At the heart of the gospel there is a rare brand of honesty. It is the courage, the audacity, to see yourself as you really are. You will never experience true grace until you believe you really are more deeply flawed than you have ever dared to admit to anyone . . . even yourself. It is only then you can begin to understand that if God really loves you still, then you are more deeply loved than you have ever dared to imagine.

In the first chapter of Mark, a leper makes his way to Jesus. Leprosy was a horrible disease to have in the first century. To have leprosy meant literally you were disintegrating, you were falling apart and everyone could see it was true. I sit in crowds sometimes and wonder how many people are disintegrating around me. I can't see it. It is not as obvious as it was with this leper, but it is no less true. You may be falling apart even as you read this sentence. Anyway, the leper makes his way to Jesus and when he gets close enough he says something very profound. He says to Jesus, "If you are *willing*, you *can make* me clean."[78] This man realized that a Savior always has to have two parts. He must have a desire to save. He must have a heart. But a heart is not enough. He must also have the power, the authority to save. A savior needs both love and power.

If I am floundering in the ocean and you are standing on the beach watching you might feel really bad. You might really want to save me, but if you can't swim you are helpless. On the other hand, you could be an Olympic swimmer but have no inclination to jump in and swim out to me to save me. A Savior must have both things. "If you are willing, you can make me clean."

Mary Magdelene stood and watched Jesus die on the cross. My guess is she cried until there were no more tears to cry. She knew Jesus loved her. She had never been around anyone who loved her the way Jesus loved her. But as she watched him writhe on the cross and then finally arch his back one last time and go limp, her own soul must have gone limp as well. He might have loved her but he could not save her. He did not have the power. That was Friday afternoon.

On Sunday morning she went with two other women to try to anoint the body of Jesus. It was something their love for him compelled them to do, and they hadn't had a chance to do it because Saturday was the Sabbath. When they arrived at the tomb they were greeted by a couple of angels who told them Jesus was gone. I think at that moment Mary's heart began to race. It raced because she was talking to an angel—who wouldn't have a shot of adrenalin at a time like that. But at a deeper level her limp soul began to stir because if Jesus was alive then she just might have a Savior after all. By the time she rounded the corner and saw a man she mistook for a gardener she could hardly think. But when the gardener said her name her heart screamed. There was no one else who had ever said her name quite like that. "Mary!" he said. "Savior!" she sang. Such is the moment of salvation.

Love at the cross when he drank the cup. Power at the tomb when he stood up and walked out. Resurrection. There are a lot of people who get the love of Jesus but miss his power. I think really religious people sometimes get his power but miss his love. If you are going to ever experience the effect of the gospel, you must have a Savior with both power and love. Grace always flows red like blood. That is why there is a cross. But for grace to have the power to save we need a risen Savior. That is why the tomb is empty today.

Rob Thomas

18

Red Like Blood Goes Live

BOB

Joe and I would like you to know that this book lives on at Red LikeBlood.com. That's where we update our stories and add new ones as they unfold. New photos and videos, too. No extra charge.

One reason we're excited about this is that many of the people you've read about here will appear on the site from time to time, in a blog post, a video, or best of all, through the Ask a Question tab. You can go there to address a question to Rita, Amy, and Karen, plus many of our friends like Tom Randall, Rob Thomas, Pastor Marshall Brandon, Tim Elliott, Jay the Pacifist, and bariatric surgeon Steve Myers. Maybe even Jerry Bridges.

And here's the best part. RedLikeBlood.com is a community where, on the Tell Your Story tab, you can share *your* stories of brokenness and grace. Like-minded readers will respond and you can carry on a conversation with them. Joe or I may chime in, or you might hear from one of the other people I just named. It's a place where you can explore deep questions. It's a place where you'll laugh and sometimes cry. Maybe you'll meet someone there and get married and have six kids. Okay, maybe not. But stranger things have happened.

Consider this your official invitation to dive into grace with us. We hope to see you there.

⁓

But maybe you're not ready for that quite yet. Maybe you sense your brokenness, but you haven't yet experienced the kind of grace Joe and I have described in this book. The remainder of this chapter is for you.

I looked back over everything I've shared in the previous chapters. It got me wondering—how did all this grace come to a person like me? I know it came through brokenness. But there's a lot of graceless brokenness out there. Why is my brokenness any different? There are people ten times smarter than me who have never tasted a single drop of grace. So intelligence has nothing to do with it. And there are people with one-tenth the education I've had who swim in grace all the time. So it's not because I took the right classes at Ohio State. I've concluded and Joe agrees: We don't get a grip on grace. Grace gets a grip on us. Ultimately, God allows brokenness, and then in his own timing, he initiates the flow of grace. In other words, we experience grace because God personally invades our lives to bring the good news of the gospel to us.

If that's true, it means God loves you so much he has perfectly orchestrated a finely tuned set of circumstances to reveal something important. Something that's true for all of us. Something we all have a hard time seeing. *He's helping you discover just how desperately you need his grace.* Because once you see it you'll be close to the place where that grace starts flowing.

My guess is your very first step toward grace will involve taking a hard look in the mirror. Take my advice. Linger there until you see the raw reality of your sin. Trust me, I'm an expert on this—I am the chief of sinners. I have sin-in-the-mirror moments on a daily basis. Sometimes they're big and sometimes they're little. And sometimes they're overwhelming. Like the moment I stood alone in the loft at the condo and four hard facts crashed in on me in a split second. First, I had left Rita, Dave, and Lauren, shattering their lives. Second, Amy had left me, shattering my self-centered dreams. Third, no amount of porn, alcohol, or pills could even begin to fill the void. And, fourth, my sin had removed any and all awareness of God's love for me. I suddenly longed to experience his love again—and here's my point—God brought me to that moment. All I brought to it was my depravity. My brokenness.

But maybe the brokenness you're experiencing isn't the result of your own sin. Maybe you're suffering as a result of someone else's sin. Or maybe there's no sin on the table at all. Like on the morning our two-month-old daughter, Grace, lay dying of internal bleeding in Children's Hospital. If difficult circumstances have broken you, no matter how it happened, I still think the first step is the hard look in the mirror. Here are four questions to ask yourself when you get there:

1. Who is my God, really?
2. Who or what is the actual object of my faith?
3. Do I truly believe God is . . . infinitely wise? absolutely in control? and in love with me to the point of death, even death on a cross?
4. Have I been trying to manipulate the God of the Universe?

These are X-ray questions. They might reveal hidden sin. If they do, meet God on his own terms at the cross, the place made just for a time like this. Remember, the gospel is only for sinners. Jesus lived and died in your place, as your substitute, so that you could run into the arms of the Father and experience love beyond degree.

What if you have all the right answers to the four X-ray questions and yet grace seems nowhere to be found? That can happen. Think of the righteous guy named Job at the beginning of that Old Testament story. Think of Tom Randall suffering from poisoning on the streets of Manila. It seems to me that, sin or no sin, there is always a time gap between the first evidence of brokenness and the moment grace begins to flow. Sometimes the gap is days or weeks. But it can be years. Sometimes you're looking for grace. Sometimes you aren't. Either way *the gap* is a tough place to be. If you happen to be close to me when I'm in one you'd sense something like groaning coming from my soul.

There was a six-month gap between the day I hit rock bottom at the condo and the day Amy and I opened the Bible and grace flew off the page. And as baby Grace's brain hemorrhage got worse by the minute, there was a 24-hour gap between the moment Amy and I realized we were absolutely helpless, and the moment they handed her back to us as an embodiment of God's grace.

Joe and I have had two very different journeys. He's a pastor's kid turned pastor. I'm a prodigal come home. But we've both learned that the brokenness God allows is always merciful and purposeful—because it's designed to move our soul to a destination where we become more dependent on God alone. And somewhere in the time gap on our way to that place, grace always begins to flow. And as everyone who has experienced real grace will tell you—it's well worth the wait.

One extraordinary day in the life of the apostle Paul, he experienced *extreme* closeness with God.[79] He was "caught up into the third heaven" where "he heard things that cannot be told, which man may not utter." But in the wake of that experience, God gave him a "thorn in the flesh" to harass him and keep him from becoming conceited. Paul understood his thorn to be a messenger of Satan. I bet the ordeal reminded him a little of the treatment Job got back in the day. So God deliberately exposes his most favored adopted sons to satanic attack? Why? God's merciful and purposeful ways are revealed in the rest of the story.

Paul became desperate. He begged God to remove the thorn. Three times. We don't know exactly how long Paul was in the gap. But he was in there for sure. Eventually God did something far better than remove the thorn. Something truly supernatural. He provided grace. Paul quotes the message he heard from the Lord:

"My grace is sufficient for you, for my power is made perfect in weakness."

This was all Paul needed to hear. His trust in the Father's love was solid. So his entire life rose above the on-going, painful, thorny circumstance. And we see glory shining out of grace-filled cracks in the very next sentences he wrote:

Therefore I will boast all the more gladly of my weaknesses, so that the power of Christ may rest upon me. For the sake of Christ, then, I am content with weaknesses, insults, hardships, persecutions, and calamities.

For when I am weak, then I am strong.

If that's not transcendent, what is? By the way, there's no indication anywhere that God ever removed the thorn. At least not until Paul was back in the third heaven after having his head lopped off by Emperor Nero's henchman.

The gap is the incubator where God grows our faith. It's the place where he helps us to see the unseen. God knows my faith is small and weak so he puts me in one gap after another. When I get in one I pray for faith. One of my favorite prayers is, "I believe, help my unbelief."[80] If I had a dollar for every time I prayed that prayer I could definitely afford to treat my mother to a second trip to Italy. Sometimes when I emerge from a gap I notice my faith has grown a little.

I'm actually in a really big gap right now. An unprecedented circumstance that's beyond my control. I see glimpses of his presence and feel trickles of his comfort almost every day, but it seems like I've been waiting forever for God to put out this fire. A year is not forever, but it's still a long time. I know that he knows the precise best moment to open the valve so grace will flow and not trickle. *How long, O Lord?*[81]

Rob came over to clean our house the other day. He listened to the gory details of my gap story and entered into my pain. His face got intense for a moment. And then his smile returned.

"You know," he said, "you're not the only one who is waiting."

"What do you mean?"

"God's waiting for you, too. He's waiting for you to come higher up and further in."[82]

"Hmm."

"And another thing . . ."

"What's that, Rob?"

"Jesus stood in the only gap that was insurmountable for us to bear. And that's never the gap we're in."

"Yeah. You're absolutely right."

"Oh. One more thing."

Rob was wigging out. He closed his eyes as grace flowed from his lips, "God, who said, 'Let light shine out of darkness,' has shone in our hearts to give the light of the knowledge of the glory of God in the face of Jesus Christ. But we have this treasure in jars of clay, to show that the surpassing power belongs to God and not to us."[83]

At this point Rob was coming unglued. And I was beginning to see the unseen. And before long, we both were reveling in liquid grace.

Acknowledgments

JOE

I would like to express my gratitude to my wife, Karen, whose strength and beauty still inspire me. To my children Jeremy, Rachel and Becca, who have been constant sources of joy. Thanks to my parents, who began a legacy of faith and first taught me to love the Savior. And to my brother, Brian, who has been my hero from childhood. Finally, I would like to thank my family at Christ Community Chapel who show me what faith looks like as it is lived out day by day.

BOB

I'm grateful for six special people whose stories of brokenness and grace are intertwined with my own: my wife, Amy, my former wife, Rita, and my four wonderful kids, Dave, Lauren, Grace, and Michael. May grace continue to confront us and pour through the cracks in our lives. I'd also like to thank four special friends who gave me valuable feedback on the manuscript: Jerry Bridges, Sandy Andrassy, Brent Lutz ("my favorite son-in-law"), and Danny Lee. And to my mother, Vivacious, I say, "*Tanto amore da tuo figlio numero uno.*"

We both want to thank all the people who have shared their stories with us and allowed us to pass them on to you in *Red Like Blood*.

Thanks to Brad Cvammen and Bob Zeller for photography, and to Zac Novak and Ben McRae for videography at RedLikeBlood.com

We'd also like to thank the Tripp family and the entire team at Shepherd Press. Special thanks to our editor and friend, Kevin Meath, and to our production manager, Rick Irvin.

Most of all, we express gratitude to Jesus Christ, the Son of God and Son of Man. You are supremely glorious and we adore you. And we thank you for your finished work for us on the cross and for the grace you purchased for us there as your blood flowed red.

Notes

1. Back then it was called Hudson Community Chapel but it has since changed its name to Christ Community Chapel. See www.ccchapel.com for more on our church.

2. From the poem, "Ozymandias," by Percy Bysshe Shelley.

3. Frederick Buechner, *Godric* (New York, NY: HarperCollins Publisher Ltd. 1980).

4. Donald Miller, *Blue Like Jazz* (Nashville, Tennessee: Thomas Nelson, Inc. 2003), 117–127.

5. Weltyde is not his real last name. I changed it here to save him from possible embarrassment and from having random people try to track him down. But if you knew Mark and I back then, you'd know his last name. And I hope you will help me find him soon. You can reach me through www.RedLikeBlood.com

6. John 8:29

7. Colossians 1:15–17

8. Timothy Keller, *The Prodigal God: Recovering the Heart of the Christian Faith* (New York, NY: Penguin Group USA Inc. 2008), 45.

9. James 1:17

10. 1 John 1:3

11. You can read the whole story in Daniel 3

12. 1 John 4:19

13. See Psalm 2:1–6

14. John 1:1

15. Psalm 135:6

16. Acts 17:24–25

17. John 10:11, 18

18. Philippians 2:6–8

19. Isaiah 30:21

20. Romans 6:14

21. John R. W. Stott, *The Message of Galatians* (London, 1968), 179.
22. John 11:35
23. http://www.desiringgod.org/resource-library/taste-see-articles/ dont-waste-your-cancer
24. Philippians 1:21, 3:8
25. Acts 7:55–56
26. Isaiah 55:8–9
27. Psalm 139:6
28. Acts 20:35
29. Matthew 23:11
30. Mark 8:35
31. Genesis 50:20
32. 2 Corinthians 12:10b
33. http://www.DesiringGod.org/ResourceLibrary/MediaPlayer/1674/ Video/
34. Romans 8:18
35. 1 Corinthians 2:9 (KJV)
36. John 8:36
37. John 4:10
38. John 10:10
39. Matthew 26:26, Luke 22:19
40. Romans 8:2
41. See 1 Corinthians 10:13
42. John 8:36
43. See 2 Samuel 11:1–12:15
44. Colossians 1:22
45. Isaiah 61:10
46. Donald Miller, *Blue Like Jazz* (Nashville, Tennessee: Thomas Nelson, Inc. 2003), 159–172.
47. Luke 16:19–31
48. Mark 15:34
49. John 10:30
50. 2 Corinthians 12:1–7
51. Philippians 3:20–21
52. The inspiration and most of the data for this section came from a message by Dr. Sam Storms entitled, "Joy's Eternal Increase: Edwards on the Beauty of Heaven." It was given at the 2003 Desiring God National Conference. This outstanding message can be accessed for no charge at: www.desiringgod.org/resource-library/conference-messages/joys-eternal-increase-edwards-on-the-beauty-of-heaven. I highly recommend it.
53. Psalm 16:11
54. 1 Corinthians 2:9
55. Psalm 37:4
56. Luke 7:22
57. See Mark 2:13–17
58. Mark 1:15

59. See Romans 5:8
60. Revelation 22:16
61. Matthew 18:20
62. Colossians 1:27
63. Revelation 19:6–7
64. Colossians 1:16
65. See Philippians 2:6–8a
66. John 19:30, Matthew 27:50–54
67. John 20:22
68. Matthew 11:5
69. Mark 4:39
70. John 21:1–14
71. Luke 19:36–40
72. John 19:5
73. Hebrews 1:3b
74. John 16:7
75. Luke 19:42–44
76. Revelation 21:2–5b
77. Matthew 20:18–19
78. Mark 1:40–42 (NIV)
79. See 2 Corinthians 12:1–10
80. Mark 9:24
81. See Psalm 13
82. C. S. Lewis, *The Last Battle*. The Chronicles of Narnia, Book 7 (New York: HarperCollins Publisher Ltd. 1954).
83. 2 Corinthians 4:6–7